Other Books by James Montgomery Boice

Witness and Revelation in the Gospel of John
Philippians: An Expositional Commentary
The Sermon on the Mount
How to Really Live It Up
The Last and Future World
How God Can Use Nobodies
The Gospel of John: An Expositional Commentary (5 vols.)
"Galatians" in the *Expositor's Bible Commentary*
Can You Run Away from God?
Our Sovereign God, editor
The Sovereign God (Volume I of this series)

Foundations of the Christian Faith
VOLUME II

GOD THE REDEEMER

James Montgomery Boice

InterVarsity Press
Downers Grove
Illinois 60515

*InterVarsity Press is the book publishing division
of Inter-Varsity Christian Fellowship,
a student movement active on campus at hundreds
of universities, colleges and schools of nursing.
For information about local and regional
activities, write IVCF, 233 Langdon St.,
Madison, WI 53703.*

*Distributed in Canada through
InterVarsity Press, 1875 Leslie St., Unit 10,
Ontario M3B 2M5, Canada.*

*Biblical quotations, unless otherwise noted,
are from the Revised Standard Version of the Bible,
copyrighted 1946, 1952, © 1971, 1973, and are
used by permission.*

ISBN 0-87784-744-4

*Library of Congress Catalog
Card Number: 77-014880*

Printed in the United States of America

To him
who loves us
and has freed us from our sins
by his blood

Preface

This is the second volume of a projected four-part series, Foundations of the Christian Faith. It is my purpose to provide a work that can be given to anyone, particularly a new Christian, who is alert and questioning and who could profit from a comprehensive but readable overview of the Christian faith. Originally I had hoped to provide this basic theology in one volume. But I quickly saw that it would extend over four volumes, corresponding more or less to the ground covered by John Calvin in the four books of his *Institutes of the Christian Religion*.

Most theologies deal first with the doctrine of God, as did volume one in this study. Its subheadings are: the knowledge of God, the Word of God, the attributes of God and God's creation. Volume two covers the Fall of the human race, law and grace, the person of Christ and the work of Christ. Volume three will consider the work of the Holy Spirit in the application of salvation to the individual, and volume four the doctrine of the church and history.

Of course, no such work will ever cover the "whole counsels of God" adequately; even Calvin's masterpiece did not. Yet there is always room to present as comprehensive and useful an overview of the Christian faith as possible, and there is always a need for Christian people to study these truths. We live in a shallow age in which doctrine is little appreciated and in which man rather than God becomes the chief measure of reality. That leads to instability and folly. Strength comes when Christian people again delve into the Scriptures and there draw near to the God who has created and redeemed them.

As usual, I am thankful to Miss Caecilie M. Foelster, my secretary, who works with me on all my books, seeing them through the various stages of production. I am also thankful to the session and members of Tenth Presbyterian Church in Philadelphia, who not only permit me to spend much of my time in such writing projects but also encourage me in this work. Some material in this book has already appeared in a shortened version in the June-August 1977 issues of *Bible Studies Magazine*.

The dedication of this book is to Christ, our redeemer. It is to him "who loves us and has freed us from our sins by his blood" (Rev. 1:5). May he be glorified in the distribution of this volume, and may many come to know him better because of it.

PART I
THE FALL OF THE RACE

And the LORD God commanded the man, saying, "You may freely eat of every tree of the garden; but of the tree of the knowledge of good and evil you shall not eat, for in the day that you eat of it you shall die." (Gen. 2:16-17)

As it is written: "None is righteous, no not one; no one understands, no one seeks for God. All have turned aside, together they have gone wrong; no one does good, not even one." (Rom. 3:10-12)

"No one can come to me unless the Father who sent me draws him." (Jn. 6:44)

1

THE
FALL

On the temple to Apollo at Delphi, nestled against a rugged mountain in one of the remote areas of Greece, an inscription summed up the wisdom of the ancient world: *gnōthi sauton* ("know thyself"). Those two words embody the deeply held conviction that, as Alexander Pope later phrased it, "the chief study of mankind is man." That is, our wisdom consists in the accuracy and depth of self-knowledge.

On one level Christianity has no quarrel with that analysis, so long as it is remembered that knowledge of oneself always involves a corresponding and personal knowledge of the God who made us. And knowledge of God will always involve knowledge of our personal need and of the salvation that he alone brings. What Christianity does deny is that we can know ourselves apart from God, that is, apart from God's own revelation of himself to our minds and consciences. True, we can know much *about* man, both male and female. We can study our chemical and emotional make-up. We can observe how we function. But we cannot know man as he is in himself. We cannot determine what we were meant to be or why we repeatedly fail to achieve that goal, apart from revelation. That is why, as Reinhold Niebuhr says in the opening line of *The Nature and Destiny of Man,* "Man has always been his own most vexing problem."[1]

The biblical perspective on the human race is the starting point for the studies in this volume. It is best understood when contrasted with the two major non-Christian views that dominate our culture.

Thinker or Machine?

The first of these competing views of man is the outlook of classical antiquity, that is, the dominant perspective of the Greco-Roman world. Classical views of man, though varying in many points from thinker to thinker, nevertheless had one idea in common: since the highest element in the human being was the *nous* or reasoning faculty, a person was to be understood primarily from the standpoint of that characteristic. A human being thinks or reasons; and that, according to Plato, Aristotle and other Greek thinkers, sets him apart from the rest of the visible world. In Aristotle the *nous* is something that comes to us primarily from without. In Plato the *nous* is the highest element of the soul. But in both of these thinkers *reason* is the crucial element in which women and men find their uniqueness.

The consequences of giving such unique value to reason are well known. First, that emphasis tends to deify reason, making it the God-element within a human being. The justification for such deification is in the essential characteristics of reason, namely, its ability to rise above what it sees, to evaluate, to criticize, to form, to create. Each can be thought of as a "godlike" characteristic. A second consequence of the classical elevation of reason is a resulting dualism in which the body becomes something evil. If mind is good, matter is bad. Hence arises that eternal conflict between spirit and mind on the one hand,

and flesh and matter on the other, which gives substance to the most characteristic expressions of Greek art, drama and philosophy.

Another strain in Greek thought, seen most clearly in the mystery religions, viewed human nature in mechanical or materialistic terms—but that was not the dominant view of antiquity.

Two more facts may be noted about the classical view, as Niebuhr points out in his analysis. First, there is a basic optimism in the classical outlook. If reason is good and man is essentially reason, then man is essentially good. He is linked to the divine at the most fundamental level of his personality and has no defect there. On the other hand, there is a strange but unmistakably tragic note in the classical perspective. Thus, in the _Iliad_ of Homer, Zeus is quoted as saying, "There is nothing, methinks, more piteous than a man, of all things that creep and breathe upon earth." Or as Aristotle comments, "Not to be born is the best thing, and death is better than life."[2] That deep and pervasive pessimism is particularly marked in the Greek tragedies. They portray man as the victim of circumstances or of his own tragic flaws, neither of which he can change. The classical world saw no meaning to history.

It is apparent that a variation of the classical view is one of the competing views of man in modern culture: simple rationalism. In harmony with the major Greek thinkers, modern exponents of this view emphasize the supremacy of our reason as setting us apart from the remainder of creation and assume that we are essentially good at the core of our beings. But the tragic element, perceived so clearly by the Greeks and Romans, is missing. Its lack does not mean that modern rationalists regard man as actually better than the ancients perceived him or that man has become better over the intervening centuries, but rather that modern thinkers are strangely unwilling to face all of reality. Georg Friedrich Hegel's theory of historical development through thesis, antithesis and synthesis leaves no room for any real stalemate or regression due to human sin. The same is true of Karl Marx's dialectical materialism and Charles Darwin's biological evolution. Each assumes unending and inevitable progression. In recent years, as an aftermath of two world wars and current international unrest, there is enormous difficulty in maintaining an unlimited optimism. War, hatred, starvation, sickness and turmoil must be reckoned with. Nevertheless, the dominant contemporary view is that such problems can all be handled, granted the opportunity for us to fully employ our reason. Only a few perceptive thinkers seem aware that the root problems of this and every age are not in circumstances alone or in lack of education but rather in the very make-up of the human being. The rational faculty is important, as the Greeks saw it to be, but it is neither divine nor perfect. And the body, like the mind, is of inestimable worth, though fallen. Such thinkers see that in all parts of our being, we are simply less than we were intended to be.

In the modern world, however, another perspective on man is competing, with increasing success, with the classical view. It is linked to the minority view of the ancients mentioned earlier, reflected in the mystery religions and in such thinkers as Heraclitus, Pythagorus and Epicurus. In this view man is essentially flesh or matter rather than mind or spirit. That is to say that the entire universe, including us, is mechanistic. There is nothing apart from matter. There is no universal mind or higher reason with which we are linked and which gives form and direction to human life. Consequently, life is the inevitable working out of basic but impersonal laws of the universe.

The modern world has various expressions of the mechanistic view. One is the deterministic stance of Charles Darwin, according to which evolution proceeds by the laws of natural selection. Another example is communism, which views history as the outworking of the fixed laws of economics and class struggle. The behavioral psychology of B.F. Skinner of Harvard University also fits this category. Obviously, as in the ancient world, there are many variations among those who hold to the materialistic nature of things, but they are united in their commitment to an essential and amoral naturalism. Man is an animal—that is the argument—and an animal is only an exceedingly complex machine.

Most people cannot be content with that kind of naturalism, just as they cannot be content with the modern version of the classical perspective. In fact, they are caught in a dilemma leading to deep perplexity. Niebuhr analyzes it, saying:

> *If man insists that he is a child of nature and that he ought not to pretend to be more than the animal, which he obviously is, he tacitly admits that he is, at any rate, a curious kind of animal who has both the inclination and the capacity to make such pretensions. If on the other hand he insists upon his unique and distinctive place in nature and points to his rational faculties as proof of his special eminence, there is usually an anxious note in his avowals of uniqueness which betrays his unconscious sense of kinship with the brutes.* [3]

Nothing in modern life explains our nature except the truths of Christianity, for both the greatness and tragedy of man exceed the comprehensions of our culture. We sense that we are more than matter. We sense that we are made in God's image, to be his companions. But we are also aware that we have lost that image and that the bond that should exist between ourselves and the Creator has been broken. Hence, "Under the perpetual smile of modernity there is a grimace of disillusion and cynicism." [4]

Where should one begin in one's effort to achieve self-understanding? Formally we must begin with the Bible, for there God reveals our true condition to us (at least according to the convictions of Christianity). More specifically, we must begin with the Bible's analysis of the Fall of man, for there, above all, we see not only what man was intended to be but also what he has unfortunately become because of sin.

Did God Say...?

According to the opening chapters of Genesis, when God placed the man and the woman in Eden to be his vice regents on earth, he gave them the maximum freedom, authority and dominion possible for created beings. They were to rule the earth for him. And there were no apparent restrictions on how they were to do it, except in the matter of the tree of the knowledge of good and evil, of which they were not to eat—as a symbol of their dependence upon God. Many foolish things have been imagined about that tree. It has been called an apple tree and an apple, the forbidden fruit, with no biblical justification. One writer has conjectured that the fruit was the grape and the sin that of making wine. That is ludicrous. Others perceive the fruit to be sex, a viewpoint that throws light upon the barely suppressed guilt with which many of our contemporaries consider that subject, but which does not at all illuminate the book of Genesis. We know that such was not the meaning of the tree, because God instructed the first couple to be fruitful and multiply even before warning them about the fruit of the knowledge of good and evil (Gen. 1:28). In fact, the command to multiply was part of the original gift to man and woman of dominion over the entire earth.

What, then, does the fruit symbolize? The answer is not difficult. The fruit was a tangible symbol of the fact that the man and woman, even with great freedom and dominion on the earth, were nevertheless God's creatures; they enjoyed their freedom and exercised their dominion as a result of God's free gift. The fruit was a restraint upon them, to remind them that they were not God but were responsible to him. What kind of fruit it was makes no difference.

We do not know how long Adam and Eve lived in the garden of Eden in an unfallen state, though Genesis gives the impression that the assault upon them by Satan came quite early, before they had been well confirmed in any good pattern of obedience. Certainly Satan had heard God's warning, "You may freely eat of every tree of the garden; but of the tree of the knowledge of good and evil you shall not eat, for in the day that you eat of it you shall die" (Gen. 2:16-17). Now Satan comes—immediately it seems—to suggest that God is not benevolent and that his word cannot be trusted.

The word of God is the issue in Satan's temptation of Eve. Satan's first words end in a question mark designed to cast doubt upon God's veracity: "Did God say . . . ?" (Gen. 3:1). That is the first question mark in the Bible. Of course in the original Hebrew there are no punctuation marks of any kind, but the question in the thought makes the question mark appropriate in our English Bibles. "Did God say . . . ? Has God really said . . . ?" The essence of sin is in that speculation.

The exact words of Satan are of interest, for the sentence goes on to specify the matter that Satan is questioning. "Did God say, 'You shall not eat of any tree of the garden'?" But, of course, that is *not* what God said. God had said, "You may freely eat of every tree of the garden; but [here is the exception] of the tree of the knowledge of good and evil you shall not eat, for in the day that you eat of it you shall die" (Gen. 2: 16-17). Satan changes God's positive invitation to eat of every tree (with one exception) into a negative prohibition designed to cast doubt on God's goodness. Can we see what is happening here? God gives the man and the woman all creation to enjoy, with one exception—and even that prohibition is explained by means of the penalty attached to it. Satan suggests that God is essentially prohibitive, that he is not good and that he does not wish the very best for his creatures.

The woman does not initially agree with the force of that argument. But Satan's skillful question puts her on the defensive, and she replies with a correct (or essentially correct) reiteration of what God had said, ending with the warning, "You shall not eat of the fruit of the tree which is in the midst of the garden, neither shall you touch it, lest you die" (Gen. 3:3).

At that point Satan replies with an outright denial: "You will not die. For God knows that when you eat of it your eyes will be opened, and you will be like God, knowing good and evil" (Gen. 3:4-5). What is at stake in his denial? Is it food? Apples? Inebriation? Sex? Freedom? It is none of those things. The issue in this first part of the temptation is simply the integrity of the word of God. Having begun to cast doubt on the benevolence of God, which the first pair had no reason for doubting, Satan now blatantly contradicts God's veracity. The issue is simply: Does God speak truth? Then we are told that the woman looked at the fruit, saw that it was "a delight to the eyes, and that the tree was to be desired to make one wise," and ate of it. Moreover, she gave it to her husband, and he ate also.

Here, then, is the first revelation of sin's nature and of what is basically wrong with mankind. Sin is unfaithfulness. It is doubt of God's good will and truthfulness, leading inevitably to an act of outright rejection. In our day we see this most clearly in two ways: first, in the myriad of outright denials of the record of God's word in the Bible, even by theologians and pastors, and second, by the almost instinctive attempt by men and women to blame God for human tragedy.

In one episode of *All in the Family* Archie Bunker is arguing about Christianity with his atheistic son-in-law, Michael, because Archie wants to have Michael's son baptized and Michael wants none of it. They argue about a number of unessential things. At last Michael asks Archie, "Tell me this, Archie. If there is a God, why is the world such a mess?"

Archie is dumbfounded. He stands stock-still for a moment, and then tries to bluff his way through. He turns to his wife Edith and says, "Why do I always have to give the answers, Edith? Tell this dumb Polack why, if God has created the world, the world is in such a mess."

Edith answers, "Well, I suppose it's to make us appreciate heaven better when we get there."

Any honest thinker will admit that the problem of evil is a great one and that it raises questions we will probably never be able fully to answer in this world. How evil could even enter a good world created by a good God is puzzling. Why God permits evil to exist even temporarily as he obviously does is also beyond our full comprehension. But one thing we can say is that evil is our fault, whatever reasons God may have for tolerating it. In the incident from _All in the Family_ it never seems to occur to Michael, Archie or Edith (or any of the writers) that this is so.

Rather than acknowledge that simple but unpleasant truth, people say, as did H.G. Wells, that faced with the world's evil we must conclude that either God has the power but does not care or cares but does not have the power. Or else he does not exist. Such expressions fail to recognize that the cause of the problem is in us and blind us to God's solution to sin through the Lord Jesus Christ.

Outright Rebellion

Nothing we have yet said, however, gets to the most important fact about sin. The most important thing about sin is to be seen in the Fall of the man, Adam, in which it is nowhere suggested that he fell through the deception of Satan. The woman did fall as a result of Satan's arguments. In fact, she fell with good will; she had come to believe that the tree of the knowledge of good and evil would make one wise, and she wanted both herself and her husband to enjoy that blessing. Eve erred and sinned in her error. But her error, serious as it was, was not duplicated in the case of Adam, nor was it as reprehensible. Adam sinned out of an attitude of rebellion against God. The distinction is noted in the apostle Paul's interpretation of the Fall. "And Adam was not deceived, but the woman was deceived and became a transgressor" (1 Tim. 2:14).

God had placed Adam and Eve in the garden to have dominion over creation (Gen. 1:28) and had given them the fruit of all the trees of the garden to eat except one. If they ate of it, they would die. Adam, however, in full knowledge of what he was doing, looked at that one tree and said in effect, "I don't care if I am allowed to eat of all the trees north of here, east of here, south of here and west of here. So long as that one tree stands in the garden as a symbol of my creaturehood, so long as it is there to remind me that I am not God, that I am not perfectly autonomous—so long as it is there, I hate it! So I will eat of it and die, whatever that means." If Adam was not deceived, as 1 Timothy 2:14 clearly states, then he must have sinned in full knowledge of what he was doing. That is, he chose to eat in deliberate disobedience of God. And death, first the death of his spirit but then also the death of his soul and body, passed upon the human race.

The Bible never places the blame for the Fall of the race on the woman. Our jokes and much of our popular literature blame Eve for getting us into sin—another example of male chauvinism—but there is never a word of blame placed upon Eve in Scripture. Instead we read: "For as by a man came death.... In Adam all die" (1 Cor. 15:21-22); and "As sin came into the world through one man [Adam] and death through sin.... Because of one man's trespass, death reigned.... By one man's disobedience many were made sinners" (Rom. 5:12, 17, 19).

The nature of Adam's Fall says something else important. Sin is apostasy, that is, a falling away from something that existed formerly and was good. It is the reversal of God's intentions for the race. We see this in nearly all the synonyms for sin found in the Scriptures: *pesha* ("transgression"), *chata* ("to miss the mark"), *shagag* ("to go astray"), *harmartia* ("shortcoming"), and *paraptōma* ("offense"). Each concept depicts a departure from a higher standard or from a state enjoyed originally.

Emil Brunner points out that, as we suggested earlier, in the Greek view the essence of evil is to be found in matter or, more fully stated, in the life of the senses. That is, "the conception of sin in Greek philosophy ... is based upon the fact that the sense instincts paralyze the will, or at least hinder or suppress it. Evil is thus due to the dual nature of man."[5] The reason is not entirely without fault, being unable to master the sense instincts quickly. But evil is in the lower element. "If this evil is to be brought into relation to time," says Brunner, "it has to be described as that which is 'not yet good,' or has 'not yet reached the plane of spirit,' or is 'not yet' dominated by spirit."[6] The biblical view reverses the matter, replacing the "not yet" by "no longer." Man was without sin, as was all creation. God created all things perfect. But man rebelled against God and perfection, falling away from that sublime nature and destiny God had for him.

This is the essential biblical note regarding sin, as Brunner points out:

> _Whenever the Prophets reproach Israel for its sin, this is the decisive conception: "You have fallen away, you have strayed, you have been unfaithful. You have forsaken God; you have broken the Covenant, you have left Him for other gods. You have turned your backs upon Him!" Similarly, the Parables of Jesus speak of sin as rebellion, as leaving God. The Prodigal Son leaves home, goes away from the Father, turns his back upon him. The Wicked Husbandmen usurp the master's rights and wrongly seize the land which they only held on a rental. They are actually rebels, usurpers. The Lost Sheep has strayed away from the flock and from the Shepherd; it has gone astray._[7]

Sin is rebellion because it is not the primary element. It is only a secondary element. The primary element is that "good and acceptable and perfect" will of God from which we have strayed and to which we are restored only by the awe-inspiring power of the grace of God in Jesus Christ.

Pride

In our analysis of Genesis 3 we have taken time to isolate the sin of the woman and the sin of the man, contrasting them in order to define the two root elements of sin as "faithlessness" and "rebellion." When we compare the woman's sin and the man's for similarities, we soon discover a third root element in sin's nature: pride.

What lay at the root of the woman's determination to eat the forbidden fruit and give some to her husband Adam, if not pride? And what lay at the root of Adam's determination to go his own way rather than follow the path God placed before him, if not pride? In the woman's case, it was the conviction that she knew what was better for herself and her husband than God did. God had said that eating the fruit of the tree of the knowledge of good and evil would bring dire consequences. It would bring death. But Eve was convinced by her own empirical observation—after Satan had raised the doubt—that the tree would actually be good for her and that God was mistaken. What arrogance! In the man's case, the same element was present. In his pride he recapitulated the original sin of Satan, saying in effect, "I will cast off God's rule. I am too great to be bound by it. I shall declare myself autonomous. I will be like the Most High" (compare Is. 14:14).

How terrible such pride is. And how pervasive—for it did not vanish in the death of the first man and woman. Pride lies at the heart of the sin of the human race. It is the "center" of immorality, "the utmost evil"; it "leads to every other vice," as C. S. Lewis warns us.[8] It makes us all want to be more than we are or can be and, consequently, causes us to fall short of the great destiny for which we were created.

Thus, we are fallen. We are not on the way up, as today's optimistic exponents of the classical view would indicate. We are not sinful by the very nature of things, as the ancient Greeks would argue. We are not mere machines, as if we could be excused on the grounds of such an analysis. We are fallen.

We are faithless, rebellious, filled with pride. As a result our only hope is in that grace of God by which he sends a redeemer, who instead of being faithless was faithful, instead of being rebellious was obedient, instead of being filled with pride was one who actually humbled himself to "even death on a cross" (Phil. 2:8). It is that redeemer and his work of redemption that this volume intends primarily to study. But before we discuss the good news of redemption, we must explore further the extent of the Fall of the human race that makes redemption necessary. We must feel the justified wrath of God that necessarily hangs over us in our rebellious state because of our inexcusable sin.

2

THE RESULTS OF THE FALL

As soon as we begin to talk about sin we run into a problem. A dislike of the subject of sin and a desire to see ourselves in a better light than the Bible presents us causes us immediately to seek ways to excuse ourselves and our conduct. On the personal level, if we are criticized for doing something, we instinctively present a defense even when clearly in the wrong. We say, "You have no right to say that" or "It's not my fault." Probably many persons never admit that they are in the wrong about anything.

We must stop here and grapple with this tendency in our nature. We must overcome it if we are to know ourselves and God. Without a knowledge of our unfaithfulness and rebellion we will never come to know God as the God of truth and grace. Without a knowledge of our pride we will never know him in his greatness. Nor will we come to him for the healing we need. When we are sick physically and know that we are sick, we seek out a doctor and follow his prescription for a cure. But if we did not know we were sick, we would not seek help and might well perish from the illness. It is the same spiritually. If we think we are well, we will never accept God's cure; we think we do not need it. Instead, if by God's grace we become aware of our sickness—actually, of something worse than sickness, of spiritual death as far as any meaningful response to God is concerned—then we have a basis for understanding the meaning of Christ's work on our behalf, and can embrace him as Savior and be transformed by him.

Well, Sick or Dead

In facing this tendency of human nature and in attempting to understand sin we must be on guard against two types of argument. They pertain to the degree and extent of sin. That is, how bad is sin, really? And, who is affected? We often hear the view—perhaps we raise it ourselves—that, although something is obviously wrong, surely human nature is not so bad as the Bible imagines it to be. After all, we are told, the biblical writers were melancholy prophets living in a grim age; they were naturally pessimistic. Their world was filled with wars, starvation, disease and many forms of economic hardship. But this is not the year 2000 B.C. It is almost A.D. 2000. We have reason to be more optimistic. We are not perfect; we will grant that. But aren't the imperfections just that, imperfections, to be considered merely as the flaws, shortcomings or peccadillos of the race?

One answer is that if human nature is only slightly flawed as that argument supposes, then it should have been perfected by now. A more serious answer is that the "slightly flawed" view is totally unrealistic. The Bible points out that our state is desperate, and we can see it to be so. Sin is linked to death in the biblical perspective and death is the ultimate enemy and inevitable victor over all. We must escape death if we sense that immortality is our rightful destiny. Again, even apart from that consideration, the tragedy of human existence is overwhelmingly visible to anyone who will honestly view the mounting starvation, suffering, hatred, selfishness and indifference on our planet. The Christian faith is not insensitive to those things although many Christians seem to be. In its emphasis upon the permeation of every aspect of our being by sin, only Christianity gives a realistic appraisal.

The uniqueness of the biblical position can be seen by noting that in the long history of the race there have been only three basic views of human nature. They may be summarized as the views that man is well, that man is sick and that man is dead. (There are variations in the first two views, of course. Optimists unite in saying that man is well, but some may admit that he is perhaps not so well as he possibly could be. More realistic observers differ over how sick he is: acutely, gravely, critically, mortally.)

Proponents of the first view, that man is well, agree that all man needs, if he needs anything, is a little exercise, some vitamins, checkups once a year and so on. "I'm all right, Jack" is the optimists' cry. Those who hold the second view are agreed that man is sick. He may even be mortally sick, some would say, but the situation is still not hopeless; with proper care, drugs, the miracles of modern spiritual medicine and the will to live, who can tell what might happen? What we need is to work hard to cure our ills. After all, we are told, even if some diseases are beyond our ability to cure now, not all are, and even the remaining problems may be solved eventually. The situation may be bad, but—well, "where there's life, there's hope." There is no need to call the mortician yet.

The biblical view is that man is not well nor merely sick. Actually, he is already dead—so far as his relationship to God is concerned. He is "dead through the trespasses and sins" (Eph. 2:1), as God warned he would be when God predicted the consequences of sin before the Fall. "But of the tree of the knowledge of good and evil you shall not eat, for in the day that you eat of it you shall die" (Gen. 2:17).

Broken Communications

What is the degree of our sin? It will be helpful to consider the threefold nature of our being discussed in the first volume of these studies.[1] There I pointed out that one thing the Bible means when it says that we are created in the image of God is that we are each created a trinity, analogous to the way in which God is a Trinity. God exists in three persons: God the Father, God the Son and God the Holy Spirit. Yet God is One. In the same manner each of us is a trinity, created as a body, soul and spirit. Yet each is one. There is a debate at this point between those who believe in a two-part divison of human nature and those who believe in a three-part division. But that debate is not so significant as it seems. All the three-part division is intended to imply is that humans are separated from the plant world, along with the animals, by virtue of possessing a distinct, self-conscious personality, and that they are separated from the animals by a capacity to be aware of God. The soul is that through which we think, feel, react and aspire. The spirit, or capacity for spirit, is that through which we pray. We worship self-consciously and God-consciously, while the animals do not.

The human being that God created was perfect in regard to his spirit, soul and body, the apex of creation. But the Fall affected each part of his magnificent threefold nature. Specifically, his spirit died, for his fellowship with God was broken; his soul began to die, for he began to lie and cheat and kill; his body died eventually, for, as God said, "You are dust, and to dust you shall return" (Gen. 3:19).

In the area of the spirit the effect of Adam's sin was instantaneous and total. When the spirit died, communication with God was broken. Adam proved it by running away when God came to him in the garden. In contemporary language this is described as *alienation,* alienation from God, and it is the first result of that spiritual death which came to us as the result of sin. John Stott calls it "the most dreadful of all sin's consequences." "Man's highest destiny is to know God and to be in personal relationship with God. Man's chief claim to nobility is that he was made in the image of God and is therefore capable of knowing Him. But this God whom we are meant to know and whom we ought to know is a moral Being," and we are sinners. Consequently, "our sins blot out God's face from us as effectively as the clouds do the sun. . . . We have no communication with God. We are 'dead through the trespasses and sins' (Eph. 2:1) which we have committed."[2]

Alienation from God is total in its effect. It has plunged us into a state in which it is not possible for us to find our way back to God unless aided by his Holy Spirit. That is the meaning of Romans 3:10-12. The apostle Paul writes: "As it is written, 'None is righteous, no, not one; no one understands, no one seeks for God. All have turned aside, together they have gone wrong; no one does good, not even one.' "

It is important to understand that each of the three main terms of Romans 3:10-12—righteousness, understanding and seeking—is defined in terms of relationship to God. Otherwise, we distort the teaching of Scripture and affirm something that is not true. For example, if we fail to define righteousness in relation to God and his righteousness, we end by saying that there is no good in us at all. That is not true when we consider the matter from a human point of view. Not all persons are as bad as they possibly could be, and even the worst have what we might call some spark of goodness. At times there is "honor even among thieves." But that is not what the Romans passage is talking about. It is talking about righteousness as God sees righteousness. From that perspective it is true that "none is righteous, no, not one." The death of the spirit has affected us deeply and permanently in our moral nature.

Sin has also affected us in the area of intellect. Again, we must not make the mistake of explaining the phrase "no one understands" on a human level, although even on that level sin has had bad consequences. Human beings do have understanding in many areas, and some excel here. We have philosophers, scientists and diplomats. Paul's words do not deny that. What they deny is that we have understanding in spiritual things apart from the working of the Spirit of God who alone gives understanding. That is expressed in 1 Corinthians as "The unspiritual man does not receive the gifts of the Spirit of God, for they are folly to him, and he is not able to understand them because they are spiritually discerned" (1 Cor. 2:14).

The third area of our relationship to God affected by the death of the spirit is our will, to be discussed more fully in the next chapter. It is referred to in the sentence "no one seeks for God." The meaning is that not only are we incapable of coming to God because of our sin and his righteousness, and incapable of understanding him because his way can be discerned only by the aid of the Spirit of God, but in addition we don't even want to come to God. Again, nearly all women and men do seek "a god," a god of their own making who they hope will fill the spiritual vacuum of their lives. But they do not seek God, the true God who reveals himself to us in the Scriptures and in the person of Christ. Jesus said, "No one can come to me unless the Father who sent me draws him" (Jn. 6:44).

In medicine there is a condition known as *myasthenia gravis,* in which the muscles of the body cannot respond to the signals being sent to them by the brain. In a normal patient the brain signals the muscles to contract by sending electrical impulses along the nerves to the muscles where they are received by a special apparatus known as the motor-end-plate. The motor-end-plate receives the signal and passes it along to the muscle. In those afflicted by *myasthenia gravis* the end-plates are missing. Consequently, although the brain sends the signal, it is never received by the muscle. Because it is not received, the muscle does not respond and eventually shrivels up.

That is an analogy of what has happened in the human personality because of the death of the spirit. In the human system the spirit was meant to play the part of the motor-end-plates. It was meant to receive signals sent to it from God. When man sinned, however, the motor-end-plate died. Thus, although the signals are still there, although God is still speaking, the signal is not received and the spiritual life withers.

When Muscles Atrophy

The illustration of *myasthenia gravis* also suggests a second result of the Fall as it affects the individual. That the muscle cannot receive the brain's signals does not mean that the muscle merely fails to respond as the brain wishes. No, the muscle itself suffers, for it withers in its inactive state and dies. Death of the spirit also affects the soul, with the result that men and women become depraved in that area also.

We see this in Adam and Eve. After the Fall and the subsequent appearance of God in the garden, we are told that the man and woman hid, attempting to escape the encounter. It was an example of their alienation from God, the first visible effect of their sin. But God calls them forth to meet him and begins to interrogate them about what they have done. "Adam," says God, "have you eaten of the tree of which I commanded you not to eat?" (Gen. 3:9, 11).

Adam replies, "The woman whom thou gavest to be with me, she gave me fruit of the tree, and I ate" (v. 12).

On the surface Adam's reply is simply a statement, and a true one at that. The woman had given him the fruit. God had given him the woman. But that is not the real meaning of the fallen man's reply. Adam is attempting to shift the blame away from himself, where it primarily belongs, onto someone else. Most obviously, he is trying to blame the woman—hardly a chivalrous thing to do, not to mention the more basic virtue of honesty. Beyond that he is also trying to blame God. What he is really saying is that the Fall would not have taken place if

God had not been so mistaken in his judgment as to have provided him with Eve.

In a similar way Eve also shifts the blame. When God asks what she has done, she replies, "The serpent beguiled me, and I ate" (v. 13).

The point is that shifting the blame is typical of the sinful nature and illustrates what happens once the connection with God has been broken. God is the source of all good (Jas. 1:17). When the connection with God is broken, irresponsibility, cowardice, lying, jealousy, hatred and every other evil descend on the race. To put the situation into contemporary terminology as we did when we spoke of alienation, we could say that we are dealing with moral and psychological *decay*.

But there is more. Personal decay inevitably has social implications. Thus a further result of the Fall is *conflict*. Was the relationship between Adam and Eve as harmonious after Adam had tried to blame his wife for the Fall as beforehand? Of course not. That was the beginning of marital conflict. Similarly, the wish to blame others, self-interest and desire for self-advancement produce conflict between individuals, races, social stratifications, institutions and nations.

Finally, the deaths of the spirit and soul, which have such dire effects, are accompanied by death of the body also. When Adam sinned, the spirit died instantly, with the result that all men and women since are born with what we may call dead spirits. The soul began to die. In that area the contagion may be said to be spreading, with the result that we are increasingly captivated by sin. The remaining part of human nature, the body, dies last. Death is universal. Paul uses this fact to show the extent of sin: "Death spread to all men because all men sinned" (Rom. 5:12).

A Doctrine Unworthy of God?
Sad and overwhelming as it is, the death of the individual is only half of the sin problem. The extent of sin as well as its

degree must be considered. Are only Adam and Eve involved, plus those who choose to follow them in their rebellion? Or is everyone involved? We might think that the universality of human misery clearly answers the question. But those who object to the biblical conception of the nature of sin ("it's not as bad as the Bible pictures it") might object again. They might argue that corruption due to sin is not universally true of the race; further, if all people _have_ been affected by sin, that is because of external circumstances rather than because of anything basically and universally wrong within. The modern attempt is to locate sin in the injustice of society's structures.

So the question is: Are all human beings affected by sin in the sense that they are inevitably involved in Adam and Eve's transgression? The biblical answer is clear. Paul writes, "Many died through one man's trespass" (Rom. 5:15). "Death reigned through that one man" (v. 17). "One man's trespass led to condemnation for all men" (v. 18). "By one man's disobedience many were made sinners" (v. 19). "In Adam all die" (1 Cor. 15:22). "All have sinned and fall short of the glory of God" (Rom. 3:23).

Careful reading of the passages from which these verses are taken, however, shows that they are referring to something more than the universality of human sin. That all people sin might be affirmed by any honest secular writer. What a secular writer is not likely to say, however, the Bible says plainly: there is a necessary connection between all individual occurrences of sin. In other words, the point is not merely that all people sin and are therefore sinners, though that is true. The point is that all sin because they are sinners. The original sin of Adam in some inevitable way passed upon the entire human race and the guilt of sin was passed on as well. The biblical view is that God holds the entire race to be guilty because of Adam's transgression.

Is anything harder for the natural person to accept than this doctrine? Guilt by imputation? It is difficult to imagine anything more offensive to ideas of human justice and fair play. Hence the doctrine has often been assailed in particularly abusive language. It is thought to be unworthy of God, outrageous, revolting, a valid reason for despising such a God forever if it should be shown that this is in fact the way he operates. It is thought by some to be so unjust that no possible defense of it could be given. But is that so? Before the doctrine of "original sin" is rejected outright, it would be well to see if it might not represent the true state of affairs.

The Roots of Sin

The truth or falsity of original sin may be settled by the answer given to a simple question: Where does sin come from if it does not come to us as the Bible declares? We see the results of sin in the various forms of human misery and eventually in death. We may agree that in many cases the misery is the direct result of our own sin or failings. The chain smoker cannot really blame anyone but himself for his lung cancer. The overeater is to blame for the weakened condition of his heart. But it is not only the chain smoker who develops cancer or the overeater who has a weak heart. Those who do nothing to bring such things upon themselves are also affected. Children, even infants, suffer. How can birth defects, colic, cancer in the newborn and other forms of suffering by the innocent be explained if not by the biblical teaching?

To my knowledge, in the whole history of ideas only two other answers have been given. One is not really an answer at all, and the other is inadequate. The first answer is the eternity of evil. That is, evil has existed from the very beginning of things, just as good has existed from the beginning; therefore all life is characterized by their mixture. But it is no real answer simply to affirm that sin or evil always existed. Moreover, it has always proved unsatisfactory as an explanation of reality because, whatever a person's philosophical position might be, he or she nevertheless inevitably comes down on one side or the other, usually on the side that explains evil as a derivation or corruption of the good. But that does not explain the universality of sin.

The other explanation has been known popularly as reincarnation, transmigration or metapsychosis of souls. It is the idea that each of us has had a previous existence and, presumably, an existence before that and another before that and so on. The evil we inherit in this life is supposed to come to us because of what we have done in those previous incarnations. It should be said in defense of this view that it is at least a serious attempt to account for our present state on the basis of specific individual actions. It thereby attempts to satisfy the basic idea of justice which we all share, namely, that each must suffer for his own sins and not those of another. But as an ultimate solution it is clearly unsatisfactory. We immediately want to ask: How did individuals get to be wrongdoers in their previous existence? Reincarnation merely pushes the question back and back without resolving the difficulty.

What other answer is there? None, except the biblical answer: The universality of sin is the result of God's judgment upon the race because of Adam's transgression. Adam was the representative of the race. He stood before God for us so that, as Paul says, when he fell we fell and were caught up inevitably in the results of his rebellion.

Representative Condemnation/Justification
There is one last problem. It is conceivable that a person might follow the Christian argument up to this point, agreeing that the doctrine of original sin is the only possible explanation of the universality of sin as we know it. But he or she might still be angry at a God who could act so unjustly. Is the objector right? Even if the biblical picture is true, should we not hate a God who is so arbitrary as to visit the judgment of sin upon all because of one man's transgression?

Actually, the fact that Adam was made a representative of

the race is proof of God's grace.

In the first place, it was an example of his grace toward Adam. For what could be better calculated to bring forth an exalted sense of responsibility and obedience in Adam than the knowledge that what he would do in regard to God's commandment would affect untold billions of his descendants. We know this even in the more limited area of one human family. For what father is there, and what mother is there, who is not influenced for good by the thought that what he or she does for good or evil inevitably affects the offspring? Parents who are inclined to drink may hold back at least somewhat if they know that their children will be hurt by their drinking. Parents who have a chance to steal might not steal if they realize that being caught would inevitably injure their family. Likewise, the knowledge of the effect of his sin upon the entire race should have acted as a restraining factor upon Adam. That must have been a powerful incentive for good. If Adam fell, it was in spite of the grace of God toward him and not as a justifiable reaction to an arbitrary decree.

Even more important, the representative nature of Adam's sin is an example of God's grace toward us, for it is on the basis of that representation that God is able to save us. Paul says, "For as by one man's disobedience many were made sinners, so by one man's [Jesus] obedience many will be made righteous" (Rom. 5:19). If you and I and all human beings were as the angels, who have no family or representative relationships, and if we were judged as the angels were judged when they fell—immediately, individually, and for their own sin (which is how most men and women think they would like to be judged)—there would be no hope of salvation, just as there is none for the fallen angels. But because we are beings who live in relationships and because God has chosen to deal with us in that way, both in regard to Adam and his sin and to Jesus and his righteousness, there can be salvation. For in Jesus we who are sinners can be made righteous. We who are "dead through the trespasses and sins" can be made alive spiritually.

The blessings of salvation come, not by fighting against God's ways or by hating him for what we consider to be an injustice, but rather by accepting his verdict upon our true nature as fallen beings and turning to Christ in faith for salvation.

3 THE BONDAGE OF THE WILL

After having described the nature of sin and its radical and pervasive effects upon the race, it is still necessary to discuss the bondage of the will. At that point the sharpest disagreements come and the results of sin are most clearly exposed.

Luther recognized the importance of the issue. At the end of his monumental defense of the will's bondage, after demolishing the arguments of the humanist Desiderius Erasmus of Rotterdam, Luther turned to Erasmus and complimented his writings for at least focusing on the crucial issue. Luther wrote, "I give you hearty praise and commendation on this further account—that you alone, in contrast with all others, have attacked the real thing, that is, the essential issue."[1] Similarly, Emil Brunner speaks of the understanding of freedom and "unfreedom" as "the decisive point" for understanding man and man's sin.[2]

How far did man fall when he sinned? Did he merely stumble? Did he fall part way, but nevertheless not so far as to render himself hopeless? Or did he fall totally, so far that he cannot even will to seek God or obey him? What does the Bible mean when it says that we are "dead in trespasses and sins"? Does it mean that we really are dead so far as any ability to respond to God or to choose God is concerned? Or do we still have the ability at least to respond to God when the offer of salvation is made to us? If we can respond, what does Paul mean when he says that "no one seeks for God" (Rom. 3:11)? What does Jesus mean when he says that "no one can come to me unless the Father who sent me draws him" (Jn. 6:44)? On the other hand, if we cannot respond, what is the meaning of those many passages in which the gospel is offered to fallen men and women? How is a person to be held responsible for failing to believe in Jesus if he or she is unable to do it?

Such questions suggest the importance of the will's bondage. They indicate how the doctrines of sin and depravity, election, grace and human responsibility flow from it.

The History of a Debate

The importance of determining whether the will is bound or free is also forced on us by the history of Christian dogma. Significant theological debates in the history of the church have centered on the issue. In the early years of the church the majority of theologians seemed to endorse free will; they were concerned to overcome the entrenched determinism of the Greek and Roman world. On one level they were right. Determinism is not the Christian view, nor does it excuse human responsibility for sin. The early fathers—Chrysostom, Origen, Jerome and others—were right to oppose it. In opposing determinism, however, they slipped by varying degrees into a kind of unbiblical exaltation of human ability that prevented them from seeing the true depths of human sin and guilt. Augustine of Hippo rose to challenge that position and to argue fiercely for the bondage of the will, at that time largely against Pelagius, his most outspoken opponent.

It was not the intention of Pelagius to deny the universality of sin, at least at the beginning. In that, he wished to remain orthodox. But he was unable to see how responsibility could reside in us without free will. Ability must be present if there is to be obligation, he argued. If I ought to do something, I can. Pelagius argued that the will, rather than being bound over to sin, is actually neutral—so that at any given moment or in any situation it is free to choose the good and do it. In his approach sin became only those deliberate and unrelated acts in which the will chooses to do evil, and any necessary connection between sins or any hereditary principle of sin within the race was forgotten. Pelagius further stated that: first, the sin of Adam affected no one but himself; second, those who have been born since Adam have been born into the condition Adam possessed before his fall, that is, into a position of neutrality so far as sin is concerned; and third, human beings are able to live free from sin if they desire to do so, and they can do so even without an awareness of the work of Christ and the supernatural working of the Holy Spirit.

Pelagius's position greatly limited the true scope of sin and inevitably led to a denial of the absolute need for the unmerited grace of God in salvation. Moreover, even where the gospel of grace is freely preached to the sinner, what ultimately determines whether he or she will be saved is not the supernatural working of the Holy Spirit within but the person's will which either receives or rejects the Savior.

Early in his life Augustine had thought along similar lines. But he had come to see that the view did not do justice either to the biblical doctrine of sin, always portrayed as far more than mere individual and isolated acts, or to the grace of God, ultimately the only fully determining element in salvation. Augustine argued that there is an inherited depravity as the result of which it is simply not possible for the individual to stop sinning. His key phrase was *non posse non peccare*. It means that a person is not able to choose God. Augustine said that man, having used his free will badly in the Fall, lost both himself and his will. He said that the will has been so enslaved that it can have no power for righteousness. He said that the will is indeed free—of righteousness—but enslaved to sin. He said that the will is free to turn from God, but not to come to him.

Augustine was concerned to stress that grace is an absolute necessity; apart from it no one can be saved. Moreover, it is a matter of grace from beginning to end, not just of "prevenient" grace or partial grace to which the sinner adds his own efforts. Otherwise, salvation would not be entirely of God, God's honor would be diminished, and man would have room for boasting in heaven. In defending such views Augustine won the day, and the church supported him. But the church increasingly drifted back toward Pelagianism during the Middle Ages.

Later, at the time of the Reformation, the same battle erupted again on several fronts. One direct confrontation was the exchange between Erasmus and Luther. Erasmus had been sympathetic to the Reformation in its early stages, for he saw the corruptions of the medieval church and longed for their correction. But Erasmus, without Luther's deep spiritual undergirdings, was eventually prevailed upon to challenge him. Erasmus said that the will must be free, for reasons much like those given by Pelagius. It was not a subject for which Erasmus had great interest, however, so he counseled moderation even though he opposed Luther.

But it was no small matter to Martin Luther. Luther plunged into the subject zealously, viewing it as an issue upon which the very truth of God depended. Luther, of course, did acknowledge the psychological fact that men and women make choices. That is so obvious that no one can really deny it. But in the specific area of an individual's choice of God or failure to choose God, Luther denied the freedom of the will as much as Erasmus affirmed it. We are wholly given over to sin, said Luther. Therefore, our only proper role is humbly to acknowledge that sin, confess our blindness and acknowledge that we can no more choose God by our enslaved wills than we can please him by our sullied moral acts. Our sole role is to admit our sin and call upon the eternal God for mercy, knowing even as we seek to do so that we cannot do it unless God is first of all active in us to convict us of sin and lead our wills to embrace the Lord Jesus Christ for salvation.

John Calvin, Ulrich Zwingli, Martin Bucer and all the other leading Protestant Reformers were one with Luther in these convictions. In reaction to the Reformation, however, the Roman Catholic Church at the Council of Trent took a semi-Pelagian position, in which the human will cooperates with unmerited divine assistance in believing. Later, in Holland, Jacob Arminius and the more radical Remonstrant Arminians revived the concerns of Pelagius in different forms. Today probably the majority of Christians from all denominations and many theological traditions are Pelagian, though they would not recognize their beliefs by that word. Are they right? Or are Augustine and the leaders of the Reformation right? Is man totally ruined by his fall into sin? Or did he fall only part way?

Freedom to Jump

As we approach this subject on the basis of biblical teaching, we must point out that we are speaking only of the area of a man or woman's relationship to God. Otherwise we will inevitably talk nonsense. For example, we cannot take a text like John 6:44—"No one can come to me unless the Father who sent me draws him"—and argue that man has no will at all. A person who objects to that for the simple reason that he seems to be able to do what he wants to would be generally right in that contention, as we will see. Actually, he cannot do many things. But he is right in enough areas to justify his conviction, unless we maintain a distinction between our relation to God and other matters.

People obviously have free will in what may be regarded as

many nonessential things. We can decide what profession we will enter. We can decide which school to attend. We can decide whether to live on campus or off. We can choose our clothes, the make of our car, the kind of food we will eat. But those are not the most important areas of life.

By contrast, there are areas in which we do not have free will. To begin with we do not have free will in the intellectual realm. On the basis of our intelligence we can make certain choices. But we cannot will to have an intelligence quotient of 160 if it is only 100. Moreover, even if we have high intelligence in one area, it does not mean that we will necessarily have equal aptitude in other areas. I may excel in quantum mechanics, for example; but I cannot necessarily excel in literary fields, just because I will it. Similarly, an individual does not have unlimited will in many physical areas. Maggie has the free will to go out for the track team, but she does not have the free will to make it if she lacks the necessary speed and coordination. Julius does not have free will to run the 100-yard dash in seven seconds, however much he would like to. Nor can he run the mile in three minutes or look like Robert Redford.

In other words, although there are areas in which individuals do make choices, those areas are limited. Nor are they even the most significant areas. Emil Brunner says that while the Fall means that we have lost our original freedom, "it does not mean that *all* freedom has been lost; man does not cease to be a subject, and his existence does not cease to be one which is based on decision. Man is, and remains a moral personality; but he has lost the possibility of ordering his life in accordance with his divine destiny."[3] There are some areas in which the will cannot function.

Now just as we do not have free will in many intellectual and physical areas, so we do not have free will spiritually. This is the heart of the "free will versus bondage of the will" debate. Adam did have free will, but he lost it. Since Adam, all women and men who have ever been born have been born into the state Adam was in consequent to the Fall.

We may illustrate what happened by imagining that Adam was born on the edge of a steep pit and that when God created him he said, "Adam, do not jump into that pit; because if you do jump into the pit, you will not be able to get back out again." As long as Adam stayed on the edge of the pit he had free will to jump or not jump. But once he decided to jump in, free will was lost in that area. He still had free will to walk around on the bottom of the pit or to sit down. He had the choice of being complacent about his condition or complaining about it. He could cry for help or be silent. He could blame himself or try to shift the blame to another. He had free will in each of those areas. But in the crucial area of ability to get out of the pit, he was impotent.

Thus did Adam fall away from God. He did not have to, but once he did, the possibility of his returning to God was gone from him. Moreover, all his descendants have been born into his condition. Some are complacent; some are angry. Some are resigned; some are anxious. Most are hardly aware of what has been lost. But regardless of their state of mind, all are in the same condition as far as God is concerned. They cannot choose him. And none do choose him until by grace God reaches down into the pit of human misery and sin, picks the sinner up, places him or her upon the edge of the pit once more and says, "Now this is the way; walk in it."

Here is a series of texts each of which tells what we, apart from the grace of God, cannot do. First, Jesus spoke to the religious leaders of his day, asking rhetorically, "Why do you not understand what I say?" He then answered, "Because you *cannot* bear to hear my word" (Jn. 8:43). His point was not that they were physically deaf, but that they were spiritually dead. They could hear but not with understanding.

Second, Jesus spoke of the coming of the Holy Spirit, saying to his disciples, "I will pray the Father, and he will give you another Counselor, to be with you for ever, even the Spirit of truth, whom the world *cannot* receive" (Jn. 14:16-17). No one can receive the Holy Spirit as an act of the will. The Holy Spirit must be given.

Third, "The mind that is set on the flesh is hostile to God; it does not submit to God's law, indeed, it *cannot*" (Rom. 8:7-8). In those words Paul teaches that the natural man, that is, a man or woman unaided by God's Spirit, cannot by his or her own will submit to God's law.

Fourth, Paul writes, "The unspiritual man does not receive the gifts of the Spirit of God, for they are folly to him, and he is *not able* to understand them because they are spiritually discerned" (1 Cor. 2:14). The text makes the same point as Paul's phrase "no one understands" in Romans 3.

If we put these texts together, they state a doctrine of radical depravity so strong that it embraces the human will as well as every other part of the human psychological make-up. They tell us that unaided by the Spirit of God the sinner is unable to hear God's Word, receive the Holy Spirit, submit to God's law, understand biblical teaching, and cease from sin. Consequently, even if every generation had a John the Baptist to go through every city and town and point to Jesus saying, "Behold, the Lamb of God, who takes away the sin of the world," apart from the supernatural work of the Spirit of God within individuals to recreate their will and turn them from sin to the Savior, no one would turn to Jesus. Nor would it be at all different if God should send angels to rearrange the stars of heaven to say, "Believe in the Lord Jesus and you will be saved." None would believe. Consequently, if any do believe—as many have through the preaching of the gospel in this as in every other age—it is because God has first of all sent his Holy Spirit to quicken their wills, open their eyes to his truth and draw them to Jesus. It is only after God does this that any are able to choose the path he then sets before them.

Why the Lion Won't Eat Hay

There is still the matter of responsibility, however, the matter that so concerned Pelagius and has concerned many others since. Can a person be responsible if he or she is not free? Doesn't denying free will reduce a person to the level of an automaton or robot? The answer to these questions is that the inability of human beings in spiritual things is not a physical inability and, therefore, they are not excused by their failings.

Arthur W. Pink distinguishes between "natural inability" and "spiritual inability" and points to Scripture as illustrating that distinction. Thus, in 1 Kings 14:4 ("now Ahijah could not see, for his eyes were dim because of his age") and Jonah 1:13 ("the men rowed hard to bring the ship back to land, but they could not, for the sea grew more and more tempestuous against them"), it is natural inability that is in view. No guilt is attached to it. On the other hand, in Genesis 37:4 we read, "But when his brothers saw that their father loved him [Joseph] more than all his brothers, they hated him, and could not speak peaceably to him." That is a spiritual or moral inability for which they were responsible and guilty; the passage explains the brothers' inability to speak kindly to Joseph on the basis of their hatred of him.[4]

An illustration may be helpful. In the animal world some animals eat nothing but meat (carnivores). Other animals eat nothing but grass or plants (herbivores). Imagine then a lion, who is a carnivore, and place a bundle of hay or a trough of oats before him. He will not eat the hay or oats. Why not? Is it because he is physically unable? No. Physically, he could easily begin to munch on this food and swallow it. Then why doesn't he eat it? The answer is that it is not in his nature to do so. Moreover, if it were possible to ask the lion why he does not eat the herbivore's meal, and if he could answer, he would say, "It's because I don't like this food; in fact, I hate it; I will eat nothing but meat." In an analogous sense we are saying that the natural man cannot respond to or choose God in salvation.

Physically he is able to do so, but spiritually he is not. He cannot come because he will not come. He will not because he really hates God.

At this point those who do not hold to Reformed doctrine will say, "But the Bible teaches that anyone who will come to Christ may come to him. Jesus himself said that if we come he will not cast us out." That is true, but it is not the point. Certainly, anyone who will, may come. That is what makes our refusal to come so unreasonable and increases our guilt. But who wills to come? The answer is, No one, except those in whom the Holy Spirit has already performed the irresistible work of the new birth. As a result of that miracle, the spiritually blind eyes of the natural man are opened to see God's truth and the totally depraved will of the sinner is turned to enable him to embrace Jesus Christ as his Savior.[5]

Why preach the gospel? Why bear a witness if individuals are unable to respond to the message apart from some supernatural activity of God within their heart? The answer is, first of all, because God commands us to do so. It is Christ's Great Commission to the church, which we would be obliged to fulfill regardless of the make-up of human nature or the success or failure of the evangelistic enterprise. Second, we preach because the gospel is itself the power of God unto salvation (see 1 Cor. 1:18), the supernatural means by which God brings forth life in the one who before hearing the gospel was spiritually dead. It is the voice of Christ which those who are his own hear and to which they respond as God grants them a spiritual resurrection.

No New Doctrine
Is this new teaching? Not at all. It is the purest and most basic form of the doctrine of man embraced by most Protestants and even (privately) by some Catholics. The Thirty-Nine Articles of the Church of England say, "The condition of man after the fall of Adam is such, that he cannot turn and prepare

himself by his own natural strength and good works to faith, and calling upon God: Wherefore we have no power to do good works, pleasant and acceptable to God, without the grace of God by Christ preventing us [that is, being with us beforehand to motivate us], that we may have a good will, and working with us, when we have that good will" (Article 10). The Westminster Larger Catechism declares, "The sinfulness of that state whereinto man fell, consisteth in the guilt of Adam's first sin, the wont of that righteousness wherein he was created, and the corruption of his nature, whereby he is utterly indisposed, disabled, and made opposite to all that is spiritually good, and wholly inclined to all evil, and that continually" (Answer to Question 25).

An understanding of the will's bondage is important for every person, for it is only in such understanding that sinful human beings learn how desperate their situation is and how absolutely essential is God's grace. If we are hanging onto some confidence in our own spiritual ability, no matter how small, then we will never worry seriously about our condition. We may know that we need to believe in Jesus Christ as our Savior, but there will be no sense of urgency. Life is long. There will be time to believe later. We can bring ourselves to believe when we want to, perhaps on our deathbed after we have done what we wish with our lives. At least we can take a chance on that possibility. On the other hand, if we are truly dead in our sin, as the Bible indicates, and if that involves our will as well as all other parts of our physical and psychological make-up, then we will find ourselves in despair. We will see our state as hopeless apart from the supernatural and totally unmerited workings of the grace of God.

That is what God requires if we would be saved from our sin and come to him. He will not have us boasting even of the smallest human contribution in the matter of salvation. But if we will renounce all thoughts of such ability, he will show us the way of salvation through Christ and lead us to him.

PART II
LAW & GRACE

*Now we know that whatever the law says
it speaks to those who are under the
law, so that every mouth may be stopped, and
the whole world may be held
accountable to God. For no human being
will be justified in his sight by works
of the law since through the law
comes knowledge of sin. (Rom. 3:19-20)*

*And one of them, a lawyer, asked him a
question, to test him. "Teacher, which is the
great commandment in the law?"
And he said to him, "You shall love the Lord
your God with all your heart, and with
all your soul, and with all your mind. This is
the great and first commandment. And
a second is like it, You shall love your neighbor
as yourself." (Mt. 22:35-39)*

*For the wrath of God is revealed from heaven
against all ungodliness and wickedness
of men who by their wickedness suppress the
truth. (Rom. 1:18)*

*The LORD God said to the serpent, "Because
you have done this, cursed are you above all
cattle, and above all wild animals; upon
your belly you shall go, and dust you shall eat
all the days of your life. I will put enmity
between you and the woman, and between your
seed and her seed; he shall bruise your head,
and you shall bruise his heel." (Gen. 3:14-15)*

THE PURPOSE OF GOD'S LAW

4

It is one thing to state a doctrine, quite another to be convinced by it and to change one's life accordingly. That is true for any biblical teaching, but particularly true for the doctrine of the Fall and human sin. Those are unpalatable teachings which we do not readily accept. Therefore God seems to go to great lengths to convince us of them.

The primary means by which God reveals sin to be sin and the sinner to be a sinner is the law of God contained in the Scriptures, and that revelation is the primary purpose of the law. A typical view of the law is that its purpose is to teach us how to be good. That is not the Bible's emphasis. It is true that the law does instruct the wicked in order to restrain evil, and it instructs even believers as one expression of the will and character of God by which they may be urged on in living the Christian life. But its main purpose is to convince us that we are sinners and that we need a Savior. It is to point us to him.

Someone has said that we are sinners in God's sight in three ways. We are sinners by birth (we inherit sin and its guilt from

Adam), by choice (we willingly recapitulate our forefathers' sin), and by divine verdict. It is by the law that the decree is passed against us. The law is God's standard before which we all fall short. Thus we are either condemned by it or are driven to the Savior.

Defining the Law

What is God's law? That question is not so easy to answer as we might at first suppose. The concept of law is complex and difficult to grasp. We get a sense of the problem even from our English dictionaries. For example, the comprehensive *Oxford English Dictionary* lists twenty-three definitions of the word *law*. The more limited *Webster's New Collegiate Dictionary* lists nine meanings plus a lengthy paragraph of synonyms. Under biblical meanings it suggests: "the Jewish or Mosaic law contained in the Hexateuch (Pentateuch and Joshua) and in Ezekiel 40—48" and, in Christian usage, "the Old Testament."

The biblical meaning is what concerns us in this study, but even so the matter is not simple. There is variety both in Old Testament usage and in distinctly New Testament ideas. In the Old Testament the simplest and most limited use of the word *law* is for the "book of the law," to be identified either as the book of Deuteronomy or, more specifically, as the Decalogue or Ten Commandments which form the heart of that book. That law is said to have been written on a stone memorial set up in Israel after the people had passed over the Jordan River at the beginning of their conquest (Deut. 27:2-3) and to have been kept within the ark of the covenant within the tabernacle. Later the word referred in a broader sense to the first five books of the Old Testament, the Pentateuch, also called the Torah. That would be the meaning of *law* in the historical books in which the earlier written law is referred to (compare 1 Chron. 16:40; 22:12). Evidently the concept broadened continually. The phrase "the law and the prophets," which appears frequently in the New Testament but which was in use before that time, suggests that the law is the whole of the Old Testament with the exception of the prophetic books. In fact in the Psalms the word seems to go beyond even that to denote the divine revelation in general (Ps. 1:2; 19:7-9; 94:12).[1]

In the uniquely New Testament references, particularly in the writings of Paul, those four Old Testament meanings are both broadened and narrowed. Thus on the one hand, *law* can refer merely to a single statute of the law, as in Romans 7:3—"But if her husband dies she is free from that law." On the other hand, it can refer to a principle of law so broad that even the Gentiles can be conscious of it. Thus, "When Gentiles who have not the law do by nature what the law requires, they are a law to themselves, even though they do not have the law" (Rom. 2:14). In Paul's polemic writings *law* can even refer to the law principle by which no one can be justified (Gal. 2:15-16; 3:2, 5).

What does it mean that we have such a variety of definition in the Bible's use of the word *law*? If the various definitions were inherently contradictory, it could mean that the Bible provides no universally accepted definition of what the law is. There is no contradiction. Rather, careful study reveals that each writer is aware of an important and formative concept of divine law in the broadest sense, a concept out of which all lesser definitions come and which gives the specific definitions meaning. In other words, the important idea is that *law* is an expression of the character of God and is therefore a unity, as he is a unity, despite the various particular expressions of law. This understanding of the biblical outlook is supported by the fact that *law* is never used of the oral Torah or of any other form of merely human traditions.

The law is one. It is important to bear that in mind for later study, as a warning against an unjustified attempt to retain some elements (the moral law) while discarding others (the ceremonial law). As Paul puts the matter in Galatians, a person must either submit to the law as a whole (and be condemned by it) or else live by a different principle entirely: by grace. The law has value for a Christian in disclosing the nature of God's righteousness and those human acts that please him. But the Christian is not *under* that law. He is under the lordship of Christ, to whom the law with its condemnation of human righteousness has driven him.

Restraining Evil

Why was the written law given? Already we have suggested two answers to that question, namely, to convict us of sin and to point us to the Lord Jesus Christ as Savior. We need to look at these more closely.

It might be thought at first glance that the law of the Old Testament has no relationship at all to those who are not God's elect people. We might argue that the law was given to Israel, not to all nations generally. That would be a mistake for two reasons. First, it would overlook the fact that not all within Israel were saved; it was always a matter of the remnant rather than the people as a whole. Yet whether saved or not, they were under what was to them at least a civil law, which prohibited certain things and affixed certain penalties. Second, it would overlook the similarity between the law of Israel and the best laws of the ancient gentile nations. The similarity indicates that although the Old Testament law is the purest expression of the holy character of God, nevertheless God's character also has been expressed in the general moral consciousness (though in a debased form). Thus there is something like a universal awareness of moral law and a sense of need for it. So there is some value to the law for non-Christians, apart from the working of the Spirit by which they are brought to repentance from sin and to faith in Christ.

In that respect the purpose of the law is *to restrain evil.* As Calvin says, one "function of the law is . . . by fear of punishment to restrain certain men who are untouched by any care for what is just and right unless compelled by hearing the dire threats in the law," adding that "this constrained and forced righteousness is necessary for the public community of men, for whose tranquility the Lord herein provided when he took care that everything be not tumultuously confounded."[2] Paul seems to be talking about this function of law in writing to Timothy: "Understanding this, that the law is not laid down for the just but for the lawless and disobedient, for the ungodly and sinners, for the unholy and profane, for murderers of fathers and murderers of mothers, for manslayers, immoral persons, sodomites, kidnapers, liars, perjurers, and whatever else is contrary to sound doctrine" (1 Tim. 1:9-10).

Those verses and others indicate that the law is something like a tether to restrain the otherwise wild and destructive ragings of our sinful nature. But if so, something else follows: the law is not the primary thing in God's revelation of himself to humanity. The law comes in because of sin, as Paul says (Rom. 5:20; Gal. 3:19). The law is good, for it is an expression of the character of God. But it is not the basis for the relationship between his creatures and himself that God desires. It is an interim thing. Thus there was a time when the written law was not given, and there will be a time when it will no longer need to function.

Revealing Evil
A second function of the law is *to reveal sin as sin* and the sinner as a sinner. The law is given to strip away the hypocrisy of the human heart, which constantly imagines that it is right before God, and to show its depravity. Paul writes: "If it had not been for the law, I should not have known sin. I should not have known what it is to covet if the law had not said, 'You shall not covet' " (Rom. 7:7). And "Sin . . . through the commandment [has] become sinful beyond measure" (7:13).

Brief summations of law occur throughout the Bible. One

was highlighted by the Lord Jesus Christ when the Pharisees came to ask him which of all the commandments in the law was greatest. Jesus replied, "You shall love the Lord your God with all your heart, and with all your soul, and with all your mind" (Mt. 22:37, a reference to Deut. 6:5). He then added, "And a second is like it, You shall love your neighbor as yourself" (Mt. 22:39, a reference to Lev. 19:18). That summation of the law places it high above ceremonies or regulations and instead fixes it to a proper relationship between an individual and God, and between an individual and all other individuals. Both relationships are to be characterized by love. That is where our duty lies. But we do not love God with all our heart and soul and mind, nor do we love our neighbor as ourselves.

The great summation of law in the Old Testament, the Decalogue, is contained in Exodus 20:1-17 and Deuteronomy 5:6-21. We will study those laws in detail in the next chapter, noting here only that no one has ever kept them perfectly. We may come to them intending to keep them. But if we are serious and really examine our hearts in the light of what we find in those laws, we are undone. Half of the Decalogue deals with our relationship to God, just as Christ's choice of the first commandment does. It tells us that we are to worship only him, that we are to have no idols (either physical or mental), that we are to keep his name holy, that we are to keep his sabbath. But we do not obey, nor did the Jews to whom that law was particularly and solemnly given. The second half of the Decalogue speaks of the relationship we should have to others, as Christ's choice of the second greatest commandment also does. It tells us that we are to honor our parents, refrain from killing, adultery, stealing and lying, and that we are not even to wish for anything that belongs to another. But we don't behave that way. Consequently, the law exposes our sin and reduces us to helplessness before God.

The law's function in exposing sin was demonstrated historically at the time of the giving of the law. At the very

moment when Moses was on Mt. Sinai receiving the commandments, the people who were to receive them were down
in the valley practicing the very things that God was forbidding. It was a poignant demonstration that God's righteousness cannot be achieved by human beings.

Some might object at this point that God's expecting us to
live up to his standards of righteousness is unjust. Therefore,
it might be argued, we should be talking not about the first
and greatest commandment or the second commandment or
even the first ten commandments but rather something more
like the Golden Rule: "So whatever you wish that men would
do to you, do so to them" (Mt. 7:12). Didn't Jesus himself
say, "This is the law and the prophets"? In answer we must
say that if the intention of that objection is to whittle down
God's standards, it is improper, impossible and foolish. God
has a right to the highest standards—in fact, no other standards are possible for him—and it is by those standards that
we will be judged, whether we consider it just or not. But apart
from that consideration, we answer that it does not really matter in one sense which standard we wish to be judged by; we
are condemned by the Golden Rule as well, because we do not
in fact do to others everything we wish they would do to us.

What about even lesser standards? What about the rock-
bottom standard of "fair play"? Why not just treat the other
person fairly? Do we do that? Do we always treat other persons
by the same measure of fairness that we would apply if we
were thinking of their relationship to us? To ask that question
is to answer it. Everyone knows that he or she does not behave
that way, at least not all the time. Consequently, we conclude
that the law, in whatever form it appears, from the highest
expressions to the lowest, exposes sin and brings its just condemnation upon the sinner. The law is, in fact, a mirror, as
Calvin notes, in which "we contemplate our weakness, then
the iniquity arising from this, and finally the curse coming
from both—just as a mirror shows us the spots on our face."[3]

Paul says: "Now we know that whatever the law says it speaks to those who are under the law, so that every mouth may be stopped, and the whole world may be held accountable to God. For no human being will be justified in his sight by works of the law, since through the law comes knowledge of sin" (Rom. 3:19-20). The law has several functions, but the one thing it cannot do is make a woman or man righteous before God. Instead, it reveals them to be guilty.

The Gospel in the Law

Although the primary function of the law is to expose sin, it is not as if God gave it to bring himself delight when his rebellious creatures find themselves to be sinful and are repulsed by it. God does not rub his hands together and say, "Well, at least they know how sinful they are. I hope they like it." No, even in the disclosure of sin a further purpose is evident: that having discovered their sin people might *turn to Christ* for cleansing from it. The mirror is provided so that having seen the dirt on their faces people will turn from the mirror to the soap and water with which the dirt may be washed away.

The fault in that illustration is the suggestion that the law has nothing to say about the solution to the problem. Here the broadest of our earlier definitions of the law, the whole of the biblical revelation, must be brought in. The law in that sense includes not merely the prohibitions before which we are condemned, but also the promise of a perfect salvation. When God gave the law, he also gave instructions concerning the sacrifices. When God chose Moses as the law giver, he also chose Aaron to be the high priest. It is as though God, in the moment in which he thundered out in the Decalogue, "You shall not . . . ," also went on to say quietly, "But I know you will, and so this is the way to get out of it."

All the Old Testament sacrifices point in one way or another to the coming of the Lord Jesus Christ. But the meaning of Christ's sacrifice was made particularly clear in the instructions for the two sacrifices to be performed in Israel on the Day of Atonement. In the first sacrifice a goat was driven away into the wilderness to die there. That goat was first brought to Aaron or to a priest who succeeded him. The priest placed his hands on the goat's head, thereby identifying himself and the people whom he represented with the goat. He confessed the sins of the people in prayer, thereby in a symbolic fashion transferring them to the goat. Then the goat was driven out into the wilderness. The description of that ceremony states, "The goat shall bear all their iniquities upon him" (Lev. 16: 22). The sacrifice points to Jesus who, like that goat, "suffered outside the gate" in order to carry our iniquities away from us (compare Heb. 13:12).

The other sacrifice was made in the courtyard of the temple, from which blood was then carried into the Holy of Holies to be sprinkled on the ark of the covenant. The place where the blood was to be put was symbolic, as was the whole ritual. It was called the mercy seat. Being on the lid of the ark, the mercy seat was between the stone tablets of the law of Moses (within the ark) and the space between the outstretched wings of the cherubim over the ark (symbolizing the place of God's dwelling).

Without the blood the ark with its law and cherubim paints a terrible picture. There is the law, which we have broken. There is God, whom we have offended. Moreover, as God looks down, it is the law broken by us that he sees. It is a picture of judgment, of our hopelessness apart from grace. But then the sacrifice is performed, and the high priest enters the Holy of Holies and places the blood of the innocent victim upon the mercy seat, which thus comes between God in his holiness and ourselves in our sin. There has been substitution. An innocent has died in the place of those who should have died, and the blood is proof. Wrath is averted. Now God looks in grace upon the sinner.

Who is that sacrifice? He is Jesus. We cannot say how much

those who lived before the time of Christ understood about salvation. Some, like the prophets, undoubtedly understood much. Others understood little. But whatever the level of understanding, the purpose of the law was plain. It was to reveal the sin and then to point to the coming of the Lord Jesus Christ as the Savior. Before God can give us the gospel, he must slay us with the law. But as he does so, he shows us that the law contains the gospel and points us to it.

5 THE TEN COMMANDMENTS: LOVE OF GOD

It is unrealistic, even wrong, to focus on the Ten Commandments as if they were the whole or even the most important part of the law. The law is a unity, and nothing in either the Old or New Testaments justifies the kind of isolating of the Decalogue that has taken place in some of the writings of the church. The Ten Commandments have assumed such great importance largely because of their value for catechetical instruction.

Still the Ten Commandments should be carefully discussed for several reasons. First, such a discussion brings the law down from the abstract position it often seems to have (perhaps even in the last chapter) to specific issues. For the law to fulfill its primary role in convicting us of sin, it must convict us of particular sins of which we each are guilty. To admit "I am a sinner" may mean little more than "I'm not perfect"—but it is quite another thing to admit "I am an idolater, a murderer, an adulterer, a thief and so on." It is at that level that the law must be applied. Second, the Ten Commandments are of particular value because they are comprehensive. In most Protestant enumerations the first four range over the area Christ covered by his "first and great commandment": "You shall love the Lord your God with all your heart, and with all your soul, and with all your mind" (Mt. 22:37). The remaining six deal with the second area of responsibility: "You shall love your neighbor as yourself" (v. 39). In Medieval Catholicism, followed by Luther, the list was arranged to give three commandments to the first category and seven to the second.

As we turn to the specific commandments of the Decalogue we must not forget their broader context. In fact, we must be careful to interpret each in light of the full biblical revelation. The following guidelines apply:

1. *The commandments are not restricted to outward actions but apply also to the dispositions of the mind and heart.* Human law concerns itself with outward actions alone, because human beings cannot see into the hearts of others. But God, who can see within, also deals with attitudes. In the Sermon on the Mount, Christ taught that the sixth commandment is concerned with anger and hate as well as with the act of murder (Mt. 5:21-22), and that the seventh commandment is concerned with lust as well as with the act of adultery (Mt. 5:27-30). The apostle John reflects this view in his first letter, arguing that "any one who hates his brother is a murderer" (1 Jn. 3:15).

2. *The commandments always contain more than a minimum interpretation of the words.* Thus the command to honor our father and mother could be interpreted as meaning only that we are to show them proper respect and not speak badly of them. But that would be too little, for Jesus himself taught that it includes our obligation to provide for them financially in their old age (Mt. 15:3-6). In other words, the commandment refers to everything that could possibly be done for one's parents under the guidelines of Christ's second greatest commandment.

3. *A commandment expressed in positive language also involves the negative, and a negative commandment also involves the positive.*

Thus when we are told not to take the name of God in vain, we are to understand that the contrary duty, to reverence his name, is commanded (Deut. 28:58; Ps. 34:3; Mt. 6:9). The commandment not to kill means not only am I not to kill or even hate my neighbor, but also that I am to do all I can for his or her betterment (Lev. 19:18).

4. *The law is a whole in that each commandment is related to the others.* We cannot perform some of the duties enumerated in the commandments, thinking we are thereby relieved of performing others. "Whoever keeps the whole law but fails in one point has become guilty of all of it" (Jas. 2:10; compare Deut. 27:26).

No Other Gods

The first commandment begins where by now we should expect it to begin, in the area of our relationship to God. It is a demand for our exclusive and zealous worship. "I am the LORD your God, who brought you out of the land of Egypt, out of the house of bondage. You shall have no other gods before me" (Ex. 20:2-3). To worship any god but the biblical Lord is to break this commandment. But to break it one need not worship a clearly defined god—Zeus, Minerva, a Roman emperor, or one of the countless modern idols. We break it whenever we give some person or some thing the first place in our affections which belongs to God alone. Quite often the substitute god is ourselves or our opinion of ourselves. It can be such things as success, material possessions, fame or dominance over others.

How do we keep this commandment? John Stott writes, "For us to keep this first commandment would be, as Jesus said, to love the Lord our God with all our heart and with all our soul and with all our mind (Mt. 22:37); to see all things from his point of view and do nothing without reference to him; to make his will our guide and his glory our goal; to put him first in thought, word and deed; in business and leisure;

in friendships and career; in the use of our money, time and talents; at work and at home. . . . "No man has ever kept this commandment except Jesus of Nazareth."[1]

But why should we have no other gods? The answer is in the preface to the commandment which also serves as a preface to the whole Decalogue. The answer is in two parts: first, because of who God is; second, because of what he has done.

Who the true God is, is expressed in the words, "I am the LORD your God." In Hebrew the words are *Yahweh Eloheka.* The reason we should obey these commandments is that the God who is speaking in the commandments is the true God, the God who is without a beginning and without an end. "I AM WHO I AM" (Ex. 3:14). He is self-existent. No one created him, and he is therefore responsible to no one. He is self-sufficient. He needs no one, and therefore he does not depend on anyone for anything. Any god less than this is not God, and all so-called gods are less than this. It is because of who God is that he can demand such worship.

What God has done is indicated in the words "who brought you out of the land of Egypt, out of the house of bondage." In their primary frame of reference the words apply exclusively to Israel, the nation delivered out of slavery in Egypt and to whom these commandments were particularly given. Even if God were only a limited tribal god, the Israelites would owe him reverence for their deliverance. But the literal reference does not exhaust the statement. It applies to anyone who has experienced deliverance, whether from death or slavery or poverty or disease. There is no one who has not been blessed by God in some area, even though one may be unaware of it and not acknowledge God as the source. In addition, the deliverance applies to spiritual as well as material matters. Israel's deliverance was not merely physical but included deliverance from Egyptian idolatry as well, a deliverance from false gods. Similarly, Abraham's call to leave Ur was a call to serve the Lord rather than the strange and unworthy gods of Mesopotamia (Josh. 24:2-3, 14).

From such a perspective the reasoning behind the first commandment applies to every human being. All have experienced the Lord's deliverance. All have benefited from the progressive advance of truth over superstition through the revelation conveyed to the world through Judaism and Christianity. But do we worship God wholly and exclusively as a result? No, we do not. Consequently, the first commandment virtually shouts to us that we are ungrateful, disobedient, rebellious and ruled by sin.

No Graven Image

The first commandment deals with the object of our worship, forbidding the worship of any false god. The second commandment deals with the manner of our worship, teaching that we are not to worship even the true God unworthily. It is a demand for spiritual worship. "You shall not make for yourself a graven image, or any likeness of anything that is in heaven above, or that is in the earth beneath, or that is in the water under the earth; you shall not bow down to them or serve them, for I the LORD your God am a jealous God, visiting the iniquity of the fathers upon the children to the third and the fourth generation of those who hate me, but showing steadfast love to thousands of those who love me and keep my commandments" (Ex. 20:4-6).

If this commandment is looked at apart from the first commandment, it seems to be merely forbidding the worship of idols. But when the first commandment is taken with it, such an interpretation is seen to be inadequate; it would be merely a repetition of the first in different words. We have already outlined the progression: first God forbids the worship of all other gods; then he forbids the worship even of himself by images.

The worship of God by images or the lesser use of images as an enhancement of worship does not seem so serious. We might argue that worship is a pragmatic question as much as a theological one. What is wrong with a person using images in worship if they are helpful to him? Some people claim that images help to focus their attention. But even if they are wrong in this, what damage can it do? The puzzle becomes greater when we note the severe warning attached to this commandment. "For I the LORD your God am a jealous God, visiting the iniquity of the fathers upon the children to the third and the fourth generation of those who hate me." Why is this matter so serious?

There are two answers to that question. The first is simply that *images dishonor God,* as J. I. Packer points out.[2] They dishonor God because they obscure God's glory. That is not what the worshiper thinks, of course—he or she thinks that the image represents some valuable aspect of God's glory—but nothing material can adequately represent God's attributes.

We have an example in the book of Exodus. Not long after Moses had gone up on Mt. Sinai to receive the law, the Israelites who were waiting below grew restless and asked Aaron, Moses' brother, to make an idol for them. They argued that they did not know what had become of Moses and they needed a god to go before them on their journey. Aaron complied, taking their gold and silver to make a calf, probably a miniature version of the bull gods worshiped in Egypt. The interesting thing about Aaron's attitude, however, is that he at least did not consider the calf to represent another god. Rather, he saw it as the Lord in visible form, as is clear from the wording of the account. He identified the idol with the God who had brought the people out of Egypt (Ex. 32:4) and announced its dedication with the words, "Tomorrow shall be a feast to the LORD" (Ex. 32:5). Aaron would probably have said that the choice of a calf (or bull) was to suggest the great strength of the Lord. But that is precisely what was wrong. A calf, even a great bull, could not possibly have represented the Lord's true strength. The Israelites were really lowering their truly great God to the category of the impotent bull gods of Egypt.

One point of the plagues on Egypt had been to show God's superiority over all the gods of Egypt. By turning the water of the Nile to blood God showed his power over the Nile gods Osiris, Hapimon and Tauret. By producing an overabundance of frogs God showed his power over the goddess Hekt, who was always pictured with the head and body of a frog. The judgments upon the land showed God's power over Geb, the earth god. And so on throughout all the plagues, right up to the judgment against the sun god Ra, when the sun was blotted out by darkness, and the judgment against the first-born of all Egypt, including Pharaoh's first-born who was to be the next "supreme god." Israel's God was not to be placed in such a category, but that is what Aaron did by making a representation of him.

The second reason why we are forbidden to worship even the true God by images is that _images mislead the worshiper,_ as Packer also comments. Thus, in the example of Aaron's calf, the result of the "feast" was hardly the kind of holy sabbath God was describing to Moses on Mt. Sinai at the time. It became an orgy in which most if not all of the other commandments were also violated.[3]

The positive side of the second commandment is important. If the worship of God by unworthy means is forbidden, we should take the utmost care to discover what he is truly like and thus increasingly worship him as the only great, transcendent, spiritual and inscrutable God of the universe. Do we worship him that way? We do not. Rather than seeking him out, striving to know him and to worship him properly, we still turn from him to make gods of our own devising. Paul says: "For although they knew God they did not honor him as God or give thanks to him, but they became futile in their thinking and their senseless minds were darkened. Claiming to be wise, they became fools, and exchanged the glory of the immortal

God for images resembling mortal man or birds or animals
or reptiles" (Rom. 1:21-23).

That is the reason for the terrible warning that closes the
second commandment. God is not jealous in the way we define jealousy and thus piqued when we disregard him. Rather
our disregard is such base ingratitude, vanity and sin, that it
merits God's judgment. At the same time, as he speaks of
judgment God also speaks of having mercy upon the many
generations of those who love him and keep his commandments.

Hallowed Be Thy Name

"You shall not take the name of the LORD your God in vain;
for the LORD will not hold him guiltless who takes his name in
vain" (Ex. 20:7). The third commandment is to be taken with
the sentence in the Lord's Prayer in which Jesus admonished
his disciples to pray, "Hallowed be thy name" (Mt. 6:9). That
petition adds a positive dimension to the negative cast of the
Old Testament commandment. The name of God represents
the nature of God. Consequently, to dishonor that name is to
dishonor God, and hallowing the name means honoring him.
Since the various names of God represent his many praise-
worthy attributes, we hallow his name when we honor some
aspect of his character. Calvin says:

> *We must, in my opinion, diligently observe the three following*
> *points: first, whatever our mind conceives of God, whatever our*
> *tongue utters, should savor of his excellence, match the loftiness of*
> *his sacred name, and lastly, serve to glorify his greatness. Secondly,*
> *we should not rashly or perversely abuse his Holy Word and worship*
> *mysteries either for the sake of our own ambition, or greed, or*
> *amusement; but, as they bear the dignity of his name imprinted*
> *upon them, they should ever be honored and prized among us.*
> *Finally, we should not defame or detract from his works, as miser-*
> *able men are wont abusively to cry out against him; but whatever*
> *we recognize as done by him we should speak of with praise of his*

wisdom, righteousness, and goodness. That is what it means to hallow God's name. [4]

The various names of God have specific meanings. *Elohim* is his most common biblical name. *Elohim* acknowledges God to be the Creator of all that is. It is the name used in the opening verse of the Bible: "In the beginning God created the heavens and the earth" (Gen. 1:1). *Elohim* formed the sun, moon and planets. He formed the earth, covering it with plants, fish and animals. He made men and women. He made you. Do you honor him as your Creator? If not, you dishonor his name and thereby break the third commandment.

Another name of God is *El Elyon,* which means "God the Most High." It occurs first in the account of Abraham's meeting with Melchizedek after his battle with the kings of the plains and his rescue of Lot. Melchizedek was "priest of God Most High" (Gen. 14:18). *El Elyon* also occurs in Isaiah's description of the rebellion of Satan: "I will make myself like the Most High" (Is. 14:14). This name emphasizes God's rule and sovereignty. Do you honor him as the sovereign God? Not if you complain about circumstances or doubt his ability to care for you and keep his promises.

Yahweh means "I am that I am." It speaks of God's self-existence, self-sufficiency and eternity; it is also characteristically used in God's revelations of himself as redeemer, for example, to Moses before God's deliverance of the people of Israel from Egypt. Do we honor him as our redeemer? Do we praise him for the fullness of his redemption in Jesus Christ?

All God's names reveal something about him, and he should be honored by us in regard to all of them. We have looked at the names *Elohim, El Elyon* and *Yahweh* particularly. But he is also *Yahweh Jireh,* the God who provides. He is the Lord of hosts. He is the Father, Son and Holy Spirit. He is the Alpha and Omega. He is the Ancient of Days, seated upon the throne of heaven. He is our Wonderful Counselor, the Mighty God, the Everlasting Father, the Prince of Peace. He is our rock and our high tower into which we run and are safe. He is the way, the truth and the life. He is the light of the world. He is the bread of life. He is the resurrection and the life. He is the good shepherd, the great shepherd, the chief shepherd. He is the God of Abraham, Isaac and Jacob. He is the God of Joseph, Moses, David. He is the God of Deborah, Hannah, Esther. He is the God of the New Testament writers and of all the apostles. He is the Lord of lords and King of kings. If we do not honor him in respect to these names, we dishonor him and break his commandment.

Moreover, our actions matter as much as our words. Whenever our conduct is inconsistent with our profession of Christian faith, even if it is a thoroughly orthodox profession, we dishonor God. Those who belong to God have taken his name, so to speak, and must hallow it by their actions. If they "commit adultery" with the world, they transgress against his great love; they dishonor the name Christian (which means "a Christ one"). Such dishonor is worse than the ravings of the ungodly.

God's Day

At no point in their handling of the Old Testament law have Christians had more difficulty than in their interpretation of the fourth commandment. The fourth commandment prescribes the seventh day of the week, Saturday, as a day of sabbath rest, but the great majority of Christians do not observe it. Instead, as everyone knows, they worship on Sunday. What is more, they do not even observe Sunday according to the rules given for the sabbath. Is that right? Can Sunday observance be justified? What cannot be done is to treat the matter lightly. Of all the commandments, this one dealing with the sabbath is the longest and perhaps the most solemn. It says: "Remember the sabbath day, to keep it holy. Six days you shall labor, and do all your work; but the seventh day is a sabbath to the LORD your God; in it you shall not do any work, you, or your son, or your daughter, your manservant, or your maidservant, or your cattle, or the sojourner who is within your gates; for in six days the LORD made heaven and earth, the sea, and all that is in them, and rested the seventh day; therefore the LORD blessed the sabbath day and hallowed it" (Ex. 20:8-11).

In general there have been three approaches to the sabbath-Sunday question. First, it has been taught by some that Christians should worship on Saturday. This is the view of the Seventh-Day Adventists, for example, and of others also. Second, there is the view that Sunday is merely the New Testament equivalent of the Old Testament sabbath and is to be observed in a similar way. The Westminster Confession of Faith calls the Lord's Day "the Christian sabbath," adding that "this sabbath is then kept holy unto the Lord, when men, after a due preparing of their hearts, and ordering of their common affairs beforehand, do not only observe an holy rest all the day from their own works, words, and thoughts, about their worldly enjoyments and recreations; but also are taken up the whole time in the public and private exercises of his worship, and in the duties of necessity and mercy" (XXI, 7, 8). Later, Reformed and Puritan theology strongly upheld this position. Third, there is the view that the sabbath has been abolished by the death and resurrection of Christ and that a new day, the Lord's Day, which has its own characteristics, has replaced it. That was the view of John Calvin, who said clearly that "the day sacred to the Jews was set aside" and that "another was appointed" for it.[5]

What is the solution? We are helped by noting several important things. First, the sabbath was a uniquely Jewish institution and was neither given to nor fully observed by any other race or nation either ancient or modern. This is not true of the other commandments; they are generally paralleled in other ancient law codes. Sabbatarians generally appeal to Genesis 2:2-3 (referred to in the fourth commandment) as showing the contrary. Those verses say: "And on the seventh day God finished his work which he had done, and he rested on the seventh day from all his work which he had done. So God blessed the seventh day and hallowed it, because on it God rested from all his work which he had done in creation." Strictly speaking, however, those verses do not say that God instituted the sabbath at the time of creation; there are other verses which teach very clearly that he did it later.

Two such verses are Nehemiah 9:13-14. Nehemiah, who had been instrumental in furthering a great revival among the Jews who had returned to Jerusalem after the captivity in Babylon, had arranged a special service of worship and re-dedication. In that service the priests led the people in their worship, saying in relation to God, "Thou didst come down upon Mount Sinai, and speak with them from heaven and give them right ordinances and true laws, good statutes and com-mandments, and thou didst make known to them thy holy sabbath and command them commandments and statutes and a law by Moses thy servant." Those verses link the giving of the law concerning the sabbath to Mt. Sinai and imply that the sabbath was not known or observed before that time.

Another important passage is in Exodus. "And the LORD said to Moses, 'Say to the people of Israel, "You shall keep my sabbaths, for this is a sign between me and you throughout your generations, that you may know that I, the LORD, sancti-fy you. You shall keep the sabbath, because it is holy for you; every one who profanes it shall be put to death; whoever does any work on it, that soul shall be cut off from among his peo-ple. Six days shall work be done, but the seventh day is a sab-bath of solemn rest, holy to the LORD; whoever does any work on the sabbath day shall be put to death. Therefore the peo-ple of Israel shall keep the sabbath, observing the sabbath throughout their generations, as a perpetual covenant. It is a sign for ever between me and the people of Israel that in six days the LORD made heaven and earth, and on the seventh day he rested, and was refreshed" ' " (Ex. 31:12-17).

Those verses portray the sabbath as a covenant sign between God and Israel; that is important, for it is repeated twice. It is hard to see, therefore, how the observance of the sabbath can legitimately be applied to any other nation. On the contrary, it was the observance of the sabbath that was to distinguish Israel from the nations, much as circumcision also set them apart.

But what about Sunday? Sunday is another day established by God, but for the church rather than for Israel and with quite different characteristics. The sabbath was a time of rest and inactivity. In fact, failure to rest had strict penalties attached to it. By contrast, the Christian Sunday is a day of joy, activity and expectation, the character of which is set by the events of the first Lord's Day, on which Christ arose. The Lord regathered the disciples, taught them, imparted the Holy Spirit (Jn. 20:22) and commissioned his own to world evangelism. The fact that Sunday was established and the sabbath abolished is seen in the speed and totality with which Sunday replaced the sabbath in the worship of the early church. In the Old Testament the word _sabbath_ is mentioned frequently. In Acts, by contrast, the word is found only nine times, and not once is it said to be a day observed by Christians. The first chapter speaks of it in the phrase "a sabbath day's journey" (Acts 1:12). In chapter 13 it occurs four times in describing how Paul used the sabbath day for his evangelistic ends, going into the synagogue to preach to the Jews who were assembled there (13:14, 27, 42, 44). Later chapters give a few more similar references (15:21; 17:2; 18:4). Nowhere is it suggested that the church met on the sabbath day or even regarded it with any special affection or attention.

However, we must not think that the fourth commandment or the Christian celebration of the Lord's Day has nothing to say about human sin or our need of a Savior. The sabbath was a day of remembrance of God as Creator and deliverer of his people. The Christian Sunday is a day of celebration of Christ's resurrection. But do we observe either naturally? Does the human heart naturally set aside time, any time, to worship and serve God and to rejoice in his manifold favors? It does not. It is neither responsive nor grateful. Consequently, we stand condemned by this area of the law also.

6 THE TEN COMMANDMENTS: LOVE OF OTHERS

At one point in his writings the great Puritan divine, Thomas Watson, compares the Ten Commandments of Exodus 20 to Jacob's ladder. "The first table respects God," he says, "and is the top of the ladder that reaches to heaven; the second respects superiors and inferiors, and is the foot of the ladder that rests on the earth. By the first table we walk religiously towards God; by the second, we walk religiously towards man. He cannot be good in the first table that is bad in the second."[1] The truth of Watson's last sentence should be evident. Just as we cannot know ourselves or others adequately without knowing God, neither can we act properly toward others without acting properly toward God, and vice versa. To serve God we must serve others. To be "heavenly minded" is, contrary to the popular saying, to be of "earthly use."

Honor to Whom Honor Is Due
The second table of the law begins with a person's relationship toward his or her parents. This is deliberate, for in deal-

ing with parents the commandment focuses on the smallest unit of society, the family, fundamental to all other social relationships and structures. Other kinds of "fathers" or "mothers" are included in the intent of the commandment. Commentators have pointed out that there are political fathers (those in secular positions of authority), spiritual fathers (pastors and other Christian ministers) and those who are called father by virtue of their old age and experience. Yet the fifth commandment has the home and natural parents particularly in mind. The commandment is "Honor your father and your mother, that your days may be long in the land which the LORD your God gives you" (Ex. 20:12). It means we should look up to those whom God has placed over us and treat them with "honor, obedience and gratefulness."[2]

The dark background of this commandment is to be found in the natural human dislike for authority. That is why the family is so important in God's economy. If children are not taught to respect their parents but allowed to get away with disobeying and dishonoring them, later in life they will rebel against other valid forms of authority. If they disobey their parents, they will disobey the laws of the state. If they do not respect their parents, they will not respect teachers, those who possess unusual wisdom, elected officials and others. If they do not honor their parents, they will not honor God.

In this commandment is found the need to discipline children, a responsibility about which the Bible is explicit. The Bible says, "Train up a child in the way he should go, and when he is old he will not depart from it" (Prov. 22:6). It says, "Discipline your son while there is hope; do not set your heart on his destruction" (Prov. 19:18).

On the other hand, when the Bible admonishes children to honor their parents, it says an equally serious word to parents. They must be the kind of parents their children can honor. In one sense children must always honor their parents: in giving them due respect and consideration, despite deficiencies. But in another sense they cannot fully honor one who is dishonorable, as for example, a drunken, irresponsible profligate. Since they can fully honor and obey one who is devout, honest, hard-working, faithful, compassionate and wise, the fifth commandment encourages all who are parents to be like that. Moreover, it enjoins such standards upon all who are in positions of authority: politicians, leaders in industry and labor, educators and all who exercise any kind of leadership or influence.

Killing, Murder, Anger

The sixth commandment has been misleading to many because of the faulty translation of *rasah* as "kill" in most English Bibles. The word actually means "murder," "slay," "assassinate"; the noun forms of the word mean "manslayer." This brief commandment should be translated "You shall not murder." Failure to understand that has led some to cite biblical authority against all forms of killing. That position fails to see that the Bible recognizes the necessity of killing animals for food and sacrifice, enemies in battle, and those guilty of capital offenses by judicial process. Other parts of the law prescribe the death penalty for some of the offenses listed in the Decalogue.

To say that the word means "murder" rather than "kill" should be of comfort to no one, however. For in the biblical perspective, murder is considered broadly, and thus contains elements of which all are guilty. Here the teaching of the Lord Jesus Christ on the Sermon on the Mount is particularly important. In Jesus' day and for many years before that, murder had been defined by the leaders of Israel (and others also) as merely the external act, and they had taught that the commandment refers to nothing more than such an act.

"But is that all that murder is?" asked Jesus. "Is murder nothing more than the act of killing unjustly? What about attitudes? What about the person who has planned to kill another but who is prevented from doing it by some external circumstance? Or what about the one who wishes to kill but does not, because he is afraid of getting caught? What about the person who kills by look or words?" Human beings do make distinctions along such lines, and rightly so, from the perspective of human law. But God looks on the heart and is therefore concerned with attitudes also. Jesus said: "You have heard that it was said to the men of old, 'You shall not kill; and whoever kills shall be liable to judgment.' But I say to you that every one who is angry with his brother shall be liable to judgment" (Mt. 5:21-22).

Nor is it anger alone that the sixth commandment forbids. According to Jesus, God will not excuse even expressions of contempt. "Whoever insults his brother shall be liable to the council, and whoever says, 'You fool!' shall be liable to the hell of fire" (Mt. 5:22). In the Greek text this verse contains two key words: *raca* and *moros*. *Raca* is a pejorative term meaning "empty," but the insult is more in the sound than the meaning. It could be translated "a nothing" or "a nobody." *Moros* means "fool" (we get our term *moron* from it), but one who is a fool morally. It is one who "plays the fool." Consequently the word has the effect of being a slur upon someone's reputation. By those words Jesus taught that by God's standards the utterance of slurs and other such comments constitutes a breaking of the sixth commandment.

Obviously this interpretation searches to the depth of our beings. It doesn't help much to remember that there is such a thing as righteous anger, or that there is a valid distinction between being angry against sin and against the sinner. Of course there is righteous anger. But our anger is not often like that; we are often improperly angry at some real or imagined wrong against ourselves. Do we commit murder? Yes, we do, according to Jesus' definition. We harbor grudges. We gossip and slander. We lose our temper. We kill by neglect, spite and jealousy. And we doubtless do even worse things, which we would recognize if we could see into our hearts as God does.[3]

Hedonism on Glossy Paper

The seventh commandment is also very brief: "You shall not commit adultery" (Ex. 20:14). In the Sermon on the Mount the Lord amplifies this commandment also, explaining that it has to do with the thoughts and intents of the heart as well as with outward acts. Moreover, he joins it to a proper regard for marriage by his accompanying condemnation of divorce. He says: "You have heard that it was said, 'You shall not commit adultery.' But I say to you that every one who looks at a woman lustfully has already committed adultery with her in his heart. ... It was also said, 'Whoever divorces his wife, let him give her a certificate of divorce.' But I say to you that every one who divorces his wife, except on the ground of unchastity, makes her an adulteress; and whoever marries a divorced woman commits adultery" (Mt. 5:27-28, 31-32).

According to Jesus' view of the law, lust is the equivalent of adultery, just as hate is the equivalent of murder. God's standard is purity before marriage and fidelity afterward.

At no other point is contemporary morality in more obvious conflict with biblical standards. The mass media uses the lure of sex to push materialism and glamorize the pursuit of pleasure. Television fills our living rooms with sex-filled advertisements. Movies are worse; even the best areas of our cities feature X-rated movies or titillating horror films. Newspapers advertise such films with pictures that would have been considered outrageous even a few years ago, and report sexual crimes in detail that were formerly avoided by at least the best papers. Twentieth-century hedonism is symbolized by the so-called playboy philosophy. The dubious achievement of _Playboy_ magazine was to take the exploitation of sex out of the gutter, print it on glossy paper, and sell it to millions by a philosophy that makes pleasure the chief goal in life—in sex as in all other areas. Hedonism is the philosophy that makes personal pleasure and comfort the number-one objective; it is seen in the pursuit of a second home, a third car, and the right kind of friends, just as much as in so-called sexual freedom and experimentation. *Playboy* and dozens of even worse magazines preach the importance of choosing the best wine or stereo as well as the right kind of sexual playmate.

The problem is not *Playboy* itself but the "pleasure first" philosophy upon which the *Playboy* empire has capitalized: What contributes to my own pleasure comes first, and in the pursuit of that pleasure no norms apply.

The mention of norms leads us to another challenge to the biblical ethic, the so-called New Morality, initially popularized by such well-known churchmen as Bishop J. A. T. Robinson of England, Joseph Fletcher, Harvey Cox, the late James Pike and others. Since the early publication of their views some of these writers have changed direction. But they once advanced an approach to morality based on two convictions: first, that the proper course of action in any given set of circumstances is to be determined by the situation itself and not by any predetermined ethical norm (even a biblical one), and second, that the only absolute in any ethical situation is the demand for love. Anything is right if it does not hurt the other person, and whether it hurts that person or not is a conclusion to be reached in the context of the situation only. It follows according to those rules that fornication and adultery are not necessarily wrong. Their rightness or wrongness depends upon whether the act "helps" or "hurts" the other person. Similarly, lying, stealing, lawlessness and other things formerly thought to be wrong are not necessarily to be avoided.

We must say in response to the New Morality that love would be an adequate guide to right action were we able to love as God loves and with full knowledge of the situation and the total consequences of our actions. But we do not love like that. We love selfishly. Besides, we do not know what the full consequences of our supposed "selfless" and "loving" action might be. A couple may decide that intercourse before marriage will be good for them and that no one will be hurt. But they do not know that for sure, and many, if not all, who have thought this way have been wrong. There is too much guilt, too many deeply entrenched patterns of unfaithfulness, and even too many unforeseen and unwanted children to make the New Morality a valid or satisfying option.

Under the impact of the drift of the mass media, popular hedonism, and the New Morality, the cry, "If it feels good, do it," has become the watchword of our age. Should that new standard be accepted? In the light of God's commandments in the Decalogue and the Sermon on the Mount, the Christian must answer No. But at the same time we must acknowledge honestly, as C. S. Lewis says, that the Christian standard "is so difficult and so contrary to our instincts" that obviously something is wrong both with us personally and with our society.[4] We must acknowledge that all are sinners and that even Christians are not automatically victorious over sexual sins and perversions.[5]

Like all negative commandments in the Decalogue, this one also implies the positive. The positive statement, as mentioned earlier, is purity before marriage and fidelity afterward. We are not pure before marriage nor faithful afterward if thoughts are to be taken into consideration, and many individuals sin not only in thought. How far we come short of God's standards! How much misery we bring upon ourselves and others as a consequence!

What Is Not Yours

The view that one should not steal is a generally accepted standard of the human race, but only biblical religion shows why it is wrong. What the other person rightly possesses has been imparted to him or her by God. "Every good endowment and every perfect gift is from above, coming down from the

Father" (Jas. 1:17). Therefore, to steal from another is to sin
against God. Of course, theft is also an offense against others.
It may harm them if they cannot afford the loss. It always
diminishes them, for it treats them as no longer worthy of our
respect or love. But even in this we sin against God since it is
he who has given value to the other person. We see an example of this perspective in David's great psalm of confession.
Although he had stolen Bathsheba's good name from her and
even taken her husband's life, David said in reference to God,
"Against thee, thee only, have I sinned" (Ps. 51:4).

We are not to think that we have kept this commandment
just because we have not broken into a home and walked off
with someone else's possessions. There are different subjects
from whom we can steal: God, others or ourselves. There are
many ways to steal: by stealth, violence or deceit. There are
many objects we can steal: money, time, or even a person's
reputation.

We steal from God when we fail to worship as we ought or
when we set our own concerns ahead of his. We steal from him
when we spend all our time in personal self-indulgence and
do not tell others of his grace. We steal from an employer
when we do not give the best work of which we are capable
or when we overextend our coffee breaks or leave work early.
We steal if we waste the raw products with which we are working or if we use the telephone for prolonged personal con-
versations, rather than for the business we are assigned. We
steal if, as a merchant, we charge too much for our product
or try to make a "killing" in a lucrative field. We steal if we
sell an inferior product, pretending that it is better than it is.
We steal from our employees if their work environment
harms their health or if we do not pay them enough to guar-
antee a healthy, adequate level of living. We steal by misman-
aging others' money. We steal when we borrow but do not
repay a loan on time or at all. We steal from ourselves if we
waste our resources, whether time, talents or money. We steal

when we indulge ourselves in material goods while others go without the necessities of existence: food, clothing, shelter, or medical care. We steal if we become so zealous in saving or accumulating money that we rob even ourselves of necessities.

The positive side of this commandment is obvious. If we are to refrain from taking what belongs to another, we are also to do everything in our power to prosper others, helping them to attain their full potential. The Lord captures this duty in the Golden Rule: "So whatever you wish that men would do to you, do so to them; for this is the law and the prophets" (Mt. 7:12).

We cannot miss seeing that this commandment indirectly establishes the right to private property. If we are not to take from another, the basis of the prohibition is quite obviously that what others have rightly belongs to them and is recognized to be theirs by God. Some teach that Christians should hold all things in common, at least if they are sufficiently spiritual, but that is not biblical. It is true that for various historical and social reasons a group of people may choose to place their possessions in common ownership, as the early Christians did for a time in Jerusalem following the day of Pentecost (Acts 2:44-45). Some may be specifically called to that, either as a testimony before the world that an individual's life does not consist in the abundance of the things he or she possesses, or because that person is particularly bound by possessions and must be free of them in order to grow spiritually. The rich, young ruler was told by Jesus to divest himself of his goods and give the proceeds to the poor. Nevertheless, in spite of such special situations, neither the Old nor the New Testament forbids private ownership of goods but rather endorses it.

The case of Ananias and Sapphira is sometimes cited in support of the communal theory, for they were struck dead for holding back from the church a portion of the proceeds from the sale of some property (Acts 5:1-11). Their sin, how-

ever, was not the possession of the property but rather that
they lied to the members of the church and to the Holy Spirit.
They pretended to be giving all when actually they were keeping back some. In that connection the apostle Peter even en-
dorsed their right to such possessions. "Ananias," he said,
"why has Satan filled your heart to lie to the Holy Spirit and to
keep back part of the proceeds of the land? *While it remained
unsold, did it not remain your own? And after it was sold, was it not
at your disposal?* How is it that you have contrived this deed in
your heart? You have not lied to men but to God" (5:3-4).

The fact that the Bible establishes the right of private property does not make it easier for us to keep the eighth commandment. It makes it harder. There is no escaping the fact
that we often rob others of what is their due and so become
thieves in God's judgment.

The Tongue Is a Fire
In speaking of the theft of one's reputation in the last section
we anticipated the ninth commandment, "You shall not bear
false witness against your neighbor" (Ex. 20:16).

This is the last of a sequence of commandments having to
do with concern for the rights of another as a proper expression of the command to love. If we slander people, we rob
them of their good name and social standing. "This commandment is not only applicable to the lawcourts. It does include perjury. But it also includes all forms of scandal and
slander, all idle talk and tittle-tattle, all lies and deliberate
exaggerations or distortions of the truth. We can bear false
witness by listening to unkind rumors as well as by passing
them on, by making jokes at somebody else's expense, by cre-
ating false impressions, by not correcting untrue statements,
and by our silence as well as by our speech."[6]

Our duty toward the other person is only half the picture.
It is not only that we harm another individual by false witness
or swearing. We also dishonor God by our untruthfulness. He

is the God of truth and he hates lying (Is. 65:16; Jn. 14:6). The Bible tells us, "Behold, thou [God] desirest truth in the inward being" (Ps. 51:6). It tells us that the one who is obedient to God "does not rejoice at wrong, but rejoices in the right" (1 Cor. 13:6). It says, "Let every one speak the truth with his neighbor" (Eph. 4:25).

That is not easy to do, as anyone concerned about personal integrity is aware. In some situations telling a lie or at least shading the truth seems almost to be demanded. In other situations telling the truth seems impossible. Well, with men it may be impossible; but with God all things are possible (Lk. 18:27). How do we begin to grow in this area? We do so when we begin to realize that "out of the abundance of the heart the mouth speaks" (Mt. 12:34) and that the heart can be changed only when it is possessed by the Lord Jesus Christ. If our hearts are filled with self, then we will inevitably shade the truth to our own advantage. But if truth fills the heart, which it will do if Christ controls it, then what we say will increasingly be true and edifying.

The Heart of the Matter

The tenth commandment is perhaps the most revealing and devastating of all the commandments, for it deals explicitly with the inward nature of the law. Covetousness is an attitude of the inward nature which may or may not express itself in an outward acquisitive act. Moreover, it can be directed to almost anything. The text says, "You shall not covet your neighbor's house; you shall not covet your neighbor's wife, or his manservant, or his maidservant, or his ox, or his ass, or anything that is your neighbor's" (Ex. 20:17).

How modern this is, and how keenly it strikes at the roots of our materialistic Western culture. One offensive element of our materialism is insensitivity to the needs of others which it so often breeds, insensitivity to the poor in our own cities and to the deprived around the world. But even more offensive than this is our unreasonable dissatisfaction with our abundance of wealth and opportunity. True, not all in the West are wealthy and it is not inherently wrong to attempt to improve our lot in reasonable measure, especially when we are low on the economic scale. That in itself is not covetousness. But it is wrong to want something simply because we see another enjoying it. It is wrong constantly to seek to possess more when there is no need for it. It is wrong to be unhappy with our limited resources. Unfortunately, covetousness is what the media seem determined to instill in us so that our extravagant and wasteful economy will continue to grow even if this means harming the economies of less developed nations.

There is another way in which we see our covetousness. Many, particularly Christian people, really are content with what God has given them. They are not overly materialistic. But they are covetous for their children. They want them to have the best and in many cases would be hurt and even feel rejected were the children to sense God's call to renounce the life of materialistic abundance for missionary or other Christian service.

Sin's Wages and God's Gift

We must not close this brief study of God's law as expressed in the Ten Commandments without applying it personally. We have looked at ten areas in which God requires certain standards of conduct from men and women. As we have looked at them we have found ourselves judged. We have not worshiped God as we ought. We have worshiped idols. We have not fully honored God's name. We have not rejoiced in the Lord's Day nor served him in it. We are delinquent in regard to our earthly parents. We have killed, by anger and looks, if not literally. We have committed adultery by thoughts and perhaps by acts as well. We have not been consistently truthful. We have wished for and plotted to get things that are our neighbor's.

God sees us in our sin. "All [things] are open and laid bare to the eyes of him with whom we have to do" (Heb. 4:13). What is God's reaction? Not to excuse us certainly, for he cannot simply condone sin however much we might wish it. On the contrary, he tells us that he will by no means clear the guilty. He teaches that "the wages of sin is death" (Rom. 6:23). The judgment is soon to be executed. What can we do? Left to ourselves we can do nothing. But the glory of the gospel is that we are not left to ourselves. Rather, God has intervened to do what we cannot. We are judged by the law and found wanting. But God has sent Jesus, judged by the law and found perfect. He has died in our place to bear our just judgment in order that the way might be clear for God to clothe us in his righteousness. The Bible goes beyond "the wages of sin is death" to insist that "the free gift of God is eternal life in Christ Jesus our Lord" (Rom. 6:23). If the law does its proper work in us, it will not make us self-righteous. It will make us Christ-righteous, as it turns us from our own corrupt works to the Savior who is our only hope.

7 THE WRATH OF GOD

At one point in *The Nature and Destiny of Man,* Reinhold Niebuhr speaks of three elements in the confrontation of God by the individual. First, there is "the sense of reverence for a majesty and of dependence upon an ultimate source of being." Second, "the sense of moral obligation laid upon one from beyond oneself and of moral unworthiness before a judge." Third, "the longing for forgiveness."[1] These three elements correspond to our knowledge of God as creator, judge and redeemer. But what is most important about them is their order. They are in that order because we obviously cannot adequately know God as judge until we know something of our obligation to him as creator. Nor can we know him as redeemer until we are aware of how dreadfully we have sinned against him and how we have thereby fallen under the shadow of his judicial wrath.

That means, of course, that we must study the wrath of God before we can properly appreciate the doctrines of redemption. But here a problem develops. In the thinking of most of our contemporaries, including many Christians, the wrath of God is looked upon almost as an embarrassment, as being something basically unworthy of God. So it is not often spoken of, at least publicly. We hear many sermons about the love of God. Scores of books deal with the power of God to help us in temptation, discouragement, sorrow and many other things. Evangelists often stress God's grace and his plan for our lives. But we hear little about God's wrath or God's judgment. What is wrong? The biblical writers had no such reticence. They spoke of God's wrath, obviously considering it one of God's "perfections." It led them to present the gospel as God's "command" to repentance (Acts 17:30). Have modern Christians missed something that the biblical writers knew and appreciated? Have they neglected a doctrine without which the other doctrines are inevitably distorted? Or is the modern viewpoint more correct?

One problem is that English words fail to capture the essence of God's wrath. *Wrath* generally means "anger," and anger (at least human anger) is not much like what we mean when we speak of God's wrath in judging sin. But language is not the greatest problem. The greatest problem is the broken relationship between the entire race and God, due to sin. Sin has produced a state in which we stand condemned as sinners but in which, because of the very sin, we fail to admit our culpability and thus consider the wrath of God toward us to be unworthy of him and unjust.

Why have Christians tended to accept this contemporary but nonbiblical judgment? The idea of God's wrath has never been popular, yet the prophets, apostles, theologians and teachers of old did not fail to talk of it. It is biblical. In fact, "one of the most striking things about the Bible is the vigor with which both Testaments emphasize the reality and terror of God's wrath."[2] The way to overcome our reluctance is to seek to rediscover the importance of God's wrath by careful study of the entire teaching of the Bible about it.

Wrath in the Old Testament

In the Old Testament more than twenty words are used to express wrath as it relates to God himself; many other words relate only to human anger. There are nearly six hundred important passages. Moreover, they are not isolated and unrelated passages, as if they were all the work of one gloomy author edited into the text of the Old Testament later by one equally gloomy redactor. No, they are connected with the most basic themes of the Old Testament: the giving of the law, life in the land, disobedience on the part of God's people and eschatology.

The earliest mentions of the wrath of God are in connection with the giving of the law at Mt. Sinai. In fact, the earliest reference occurs just two chapters after the account of the giving of the Ten Commandments. "You shall not afflict any widow or orphan. If you do afflict them, and they cry out to me, I will surely hear their cry; and my wrath will burn, and I will kill you with the sword, and your wives shall become widows and your children fatherless" (Ex. 22:22-24). Ten chapters later, in a passage about the sin of the people in making and worshiping the golden calf, God and Moses discuss wrath. God says, "Now therefore let me alone, that my wrath may burn hot against them and I may consume them." And Moses pleads, "O LORD, why does thy wrath burn hot against thy people, whom thou hast brought forth out of the land of Egypt with great power and with a mighty hand? Why should the Egyptians say, 'With evil intent did he bring them forth, to slay them in the mountains, and to consume them from the face of the earth'? Turn from thy fierce wrath, and repent of this evil against thy people" (Ex. 32:10-12).

It is evident in this passage that Moses' appeal to God is not based either on imagined innocence of the people (they were not innocent, and Moses knew it), nor on the thought that wrath was unworthy of God. Moses appeals only on the basis of God's name and how his acts would be misconstrued by the heathen. No doubt is expressed that wrath is a proper reaction of God's holy character against sin.

The first uniquely biblical characteristic of the divine wrath is a characteristic that immediately sets it off from the wrath displayed by heathen deities: its *consistency*. God's wrath is not arbitrary, as if God for some minor matter or according to his own caprice simply turns against those whom he had formerly loved and favored. On the contrary, wrath is God's consistent and unyielding resistance to sin and evil. In the first passage it is wrath brought on by sin against others, widows and orphans. In the second passage it is wrath brought on by sins against God.

Other examples may be given. In the last chapter of the book of Job, God's wrath is provoked against Job's friends because of their foolish and arrogant counsel (Job 42:7). Deuteronomy 29:23-28 speaks of the outpouring of God's wrath against Sodom and Gomorrah and other cities because of their idolatry. In Deuteronomy 11:16-17 the sin is likewise described as serving "other gods" and worshiping them. Ezra speaks of the wrath of God being against "all that forsake him" (Ezra 8:22).

Something else is evident in these passages. Because the sin which calls forth the wrath of God is essentially a turning away from him or rejecting him, wrath is something human beings *choose for themselves*. We may say that the wrath of God is that perfection of the divine nature into which we throw ourselves by our rebellion. That does not mean, of course, that the wrath of God is passive, for it works actively now and will do so in perfect measure at the final judgment. But it does mean that wrath is a side of the divine nature that we need not have discovered; having once discovered it, we find it as real as all other sides of God's nature. We are not able to shut God out, even by sin. All we do is exchange one relationship to God for another. If we will not have God's love and grace, we will have God's wrath. For God cannot look tolerantly upon evil.

The wrath of God always has *a judicial element* to it. Thus, since it is evident that justice is never fully attained in this world (for whatever reason), the Old Testament writers tend to look toward the future day of the perfect outpouring of God's wrath against sin, when all accounts will be settled. We find repeated reference to "the day of God's wrath" or judgment. The first chapter of Nahum is an example.

> *The LORD is a jealous God and avenging,*
>   *the LORD is avenging and wrathful;*
> *the LORD takes vengeance on his adversaries*
>   *and keeps wrath for his enemies.*
> *The LORD is slow to anger and of great might,*
>   *and the LORD will by no means clear the guilty....*
> *Who can stand before his indignation?*
>   *Who can endure the heat of his anger?*
> *His wrath is poured out like fire,*
>   *and the rocks are broken asunder by him.*
> *The LORD is good,*
>   *a stronghold in the day of trouble;*
>   *he knows those who take refuge in him.*
> *But with an overflowing flood he will make a full end of his adversaries. (Nahum 1:2-3, 6-8)*

The second psalm speaks of God's wrath being directed against the pagan nations in that day.

> *[The Lord] will speak to them in his wrath,*
>   *and terrify them in his fury, saying,*
> *"I have set my king*
>   *on Zion, my holy hill."*
> *I will tell of the decree of the LORD:*
> *He said to me, "You are my son,*
>   *today I have begotten you.*
> *Ask of me, and I will make the nations your heritage,*
>   *and the ends of the earth your possession.*
> *You shall break them with a rod of iron,*
>   *and dash them in pieces like a potter's vessel." (Ps. 2:5-9)*

Amos directs God's warning against those who are nominally religious, who think wrongly that the day of God's wrath will be a day of their own vindication.

Woe to you who desire the day of the LORD!
    Why would you have the day of the LORD?
It is darkness, and not light;
    as if a man fled from a lion,
    and a bear met him;
or went into the house and leaned with his hand against the wall,
    and a serpent bit him.
Is not the day of the LORD darkness, and not light,
    and gloom with no brightness in it? (Amos 5:18-20)

Because of the accumulation of sin and the increasing need for a final and retributive justice, there is increasing emphasis upon the future day of God's wrath in the later books of the Old Testament.

Wrath in the New Testament

Examination of the smaller number of passages in the New Testament dealing with the wrath of God shows that it was as real for Jesus and the New Testament writers as for the writers of the Old Testament.

The Greek New Testament has only two main words for *wrath.* One word is *thumos,* from a root (*thuō*) which means "to rush along fiercely," "to be in a heat of violence" or "to breathe violently." Its unique meaning would be "a panting rage." The other word is *orgē,* which comes from a quite different root. Its root (*orgaō*) means "to grow ripe for something"; the noun form denotes wrath that has been slowly building over a long period of time. In many usages the two words have apparently lost those early distinctions and are used interchangeably. But where there is a distinction, *orgē* is best suited to denote God's wrath in that it depicts a gradually building and intensifying opposition to sin. Leon Morris notes that, outside the book of Revelation, *thumos* is used only once of God's anger.

He concludes, "The biblical writers habitually use for the divine wrath a word which denotes not so much a sudden flaring up of passion which is soon over, as a strong and settled opposition to all that is evil arising out of God's very nature."[3]

The New Testament writers speak of "the wrath to come." There is widespread recognition in the New Testament that we live in a day of God's grace, a day characterized by the free offer of the gospel of salvation through faith in Jesus Christ. Yet that does not mean that God has ceased to be wrathful toward sin or that he will not yet show forth wrath in the future day of his judgment. Rather, one's apprehension of that day is intensified. Jesus frequently spoke of hell. He warned of the consequences of sin and of God's just and certain punishment of ungodly persons. The author of Hebrews wrote, "A man who has violated the law of Moses dies without mercy at the testimony of two or three witnesses. How much worse punishment do you think will be deserved by the man who has spurned the Son of God, and profaned the blood of the covenant by which he was sanctified, and outraged the Spirit of grace? For we know him who said, 'Vengeance is mine, I will repay.' And again, 'The Lord will judge his people.' It is a fearful thing to fall into the hands of the living God" (Heb. 10: 28-31).

But the New Testament revelation of the wrath of God also pertains to the present, just as it did in the Old Testament. Romans 1:18 uses the present tense: "For the wrath of God is revealed from heaven against all ungodliness and wickedness of men who by their wickedness suppress the truth." If the tense of the verb were future, that too would make sense. It would refer to the future day of God's final judgment. But in the present tense, the verse seems to refer to a continuing disclosure of the wrath of God against wickedness at all periods of history and in all places—in other words, to the kind of outworking of the effects of sin discussed in the remainder of

the chapter. The effects include a darkening of the understanding wherever the truth about God is rejected (1:21).
They include the debasement of one's religious awareness
and a corresponding debasement of one's person (1:23),
sexual perversions, lies, envies, hatred, murder, strife, deceit,
disobedience to parents and other consequences (1:24-31).
Nothing in these lists suggests that the apostle Paul was sub-
stituting a present, mechanical outworking of the effects of
sin for a personal, direct manifestation of the wrath of God at
some future day, as some contemporary theologians have
taught.[4] Paul, too, speaks of a future day of wrath (Rom.
2:5, 1 Thess. 1:10; 2:16; 5:9). However, Paul sees the evidence
of that future wrath in sin's present effects.

We can say that God has warned us of judgment to come:
first, by our own awareness of right and wrong, of justice and
injustice; and second, by the evidences of an inevitable outworking of God's justice even now. Paul described that process
as he witnessed it in paganism. There are parallel evidences
today. For when men and women give up God, God gives
them up to "impurity . . . dishonorable passions . . . [and] a
base mind" (Rom. 1:24, 26, 28). We see it in the progressive
moral decline of Western civilization, the breakup of families,
insanity and other forms of psychological disintegration. We
see it in our own lives in such supposedly minor things as
restlessness, insomnia, a feeling of being unfulfilled and un-
happiness.

To sum up these matters, on the one hand we have the basic
and almost universal reaction of the human race against the
idea of God's wrath. It is considered ignoble of God, perhaps
even vindictive and cruel. On the other hand we have the
whole of the biblical revelation in which the wrath of God is
accepted as one of his perfections. His wrath is portrayed as
being consistent in its opposition to evil, as being judicial, as
being an aspect of God that human beings choose for themselves and (no less important) as being something about which

we have been clearly warned.

The wrath of God is not ignoble. Rather, it is too noble, too just, too perfect—it is this that bothers us. In human affairs we rightly value justice and the "wrath" of the judicial system, for they protect us. If by chance we ourselves run afoul of the law, there is always the chance that we can cop a plea, escape on a technicality or plead guilty to some lesser offense and be excused for it. But we cannot do that with God. With him we deal not with the imperfections of human justice but with the perfections of divine justice. We deal with the one to whom not only actions but also thoughts and intentions are visible. Who can escape such justice? Who can stand before such an unyielding judge? No one. Sensing this truth we therefore resent God's justice and deny its reality in every way we can.

Yet we must not deny it. If we do, we will never see our spiritual need, as we must if we are to turn to the Lord Jesus Christ as our Savior. If we do not turn to him, we will never truly know God nor come to see ourselves adequately. It is only when we know God as creator that we can discern him as judge. And it is only as we acknowledge him as judge that we can discover him to be our redeemer.

Satisfying God's Wrath

We must go on to consider the revelation of God as redeemer in the Old and New Testaments. This will occupy us in the next chapter (for the Old Testament) and then in the rest of this volume (for the New Testament) as we deal with the person and work of Jesus Christ. Before that, however, we must again look at that exchange between God and Moses over the sin of Israel. In a sense, that passage comes between the declaration of the wrath of God against sin and the subsequent revelation of God's way of salvation.

Moses had been up in the mountain for forty days receiving the law. As the days had stretched into weeks, the restless people waiting below had eventually prevailed upon Moses' brother Aaron to make a substitute god for them. Now, knowing what was going on in the valley, God interrupted his giving of the law to tell Moses what the people were doing and to send Moses back down to them.

It was an ironic situation. God had just given Moses the Ten Commandments. They had begun, "I am the LORD your God, who brought you out of the land of Egypt, out of the house of bondage. You shall have no other gods before me. You shall not make yourself a graven image, or any likeness of anything that is in heaven above, or that is in the earth beneath, or that is in the water under the earth; you shall not bow down to them or serve them; for I the LORD your God am a jealous God, visiting the iniquity of the fathers upon the children to the third and the fourth generation of those who hate me, but showing steadfast love to thousands of those who love me and keep my commandments" (Ex. 20:2-6). While God was giving these words, the people whom he had saved from slavery in Egypt were doing precisely what he was prohibiting. Not only that, they were also committing adultery, lying, coveting, dishonoring their parents and no doubt breaking all the other commandments. At that point, when God declared his intention to judge the people immediately and totally, Moses interceded for them in the words referred to earlier.

At last Moses started down the mountain to deal with the people. Even on a human level and quite apart from any thought of God's grace, sin must be judged. So Moses began to deal with it in the best way he knew. First, he rebuked Aaron publicly. Then he called for any who still remained on the side of the Lord to separate themselves from the others and stand beside him. The tribe of Levi responded. At Moses' command they were sent forth into the camp to execute those who had led the rebellion. The chapter says that three thousand men died, approximately one-half per cent of the six hundred thousand who left Egypt at the Exodus (Ex. 12:37; 32:28; with women and children, the total number in the Exodus may have been two million). At the same time Moses also destroyed the golden calf. He ground it up, mixed it with water, and made the people drink it.

From a human point of view Moses had dealt with the sin. The leaders were punished. Aaron was rebuked. The allegiance of the people was at least temporarily reclaimed. All seemed to be well. But Moses stood in a special relationship to God as well as in a special relationship to the people. God still waited in wrath upon the mountain. What was Moses to do? For theologians sitting in a library somewhere the idea of the wrath of God may seem to be no more than speculation. But Moses was no armchair theologian. He had been talking with that God. He had heard his voice. By that time not all of the law had been given, but Moses had received enough of it to know something of the horror of sin and of the uncompromising nature of God's righteousness. Hadn't God said, "You shall have no other gods before me"? Hadn't he promised to visit the iniquity of the fathers upon the children to the third and fourth generations? Who was Moses to think that the limited judgment he had begun would satisfy the holiness of such a God?

The night passed, and the morning came when Moses was to reascend the mountain. He had been thinking during the night. Some time during the night a way that might possibly divert the wrath of God against the people had come to him. He remembered the sacrifices of the Hebrew patriarchs and the newly instituted sacrifice of the Passover. Certainly God had shown by such sacrifices that he was prepared to accept an innocent substitute in place of the just death of the sinner. His wrath could sometimes fall on the substitute. Perhaps God would accept. . . . When morning came, Moses ascended the mountain with great determination.

Reaching the top, he began to speak to God. It must have been in great anguish, for the Hebrew text is uneven and

Moses' second sentence breaks off without ending, indicated by a dash in the middle of Exodus 32:32. It is a strangled cry, a sob welling up from the heart of a man who is asking to be damned if that could mean the salvation of the people he had come to love. "So Moses returned to the LORD and said, 'Alas, this people have sinned a great sin; they have made for themselves gods of gold. But now, if thou wilt forgive their sin—and if not, blot me, I pray thee, out of thy book which thou hast written' " (Ex. 32:31-32).

Moses was offering to take the place of his people as a recipient of God's judgment, to be separated from God instead of them. On the preceding day, before Moses had come down the mountain, God had said something that could have been a great temptation. If Moses would agree, God would destroy the people for their sin and would begin again to make a new Jewish nation from Moses (32:10). Even then Moses had rejected the offer. But after having been with his people and being reminded of his love for them, his answer, again negative, rises to even greater heights. God had said, "I will destroy them and make a great nation of you." Moses says, "No, rather destroy me and save them."

Moses lived in the early years of God's revelation to his people, and at that point probably understood very little. Certainly he did not know, as we know, that what he had prayed for could not be. Moses offered to give himself for his people to save them. But Moses could not even save himself, let alone save them; for he too was a sinner. He had once even committed murder, thus breaking the sixth commandment. He could not substitute for his people. He could not die for them.

But there is one who could. Thus, "When the time had fully come, God sent forth his Son, born of woman, born under the law, to redeem those who were under the law, so that we might receive adoption as sons" (Gal. 4:4-5). Jesus' death was not just for those who believed in Old Testament times, for those who sinned in the wilderness and for their successors. It was also for us who live today, both Jews and Gentiles. On the basis of Christ's death, in which he himself received the full judicial outpouring of God's wrath against sin, those who believe now come to experience not wrath (though we richly deserve it) but grace abounding. This is the day of God's grace.

Grace does not eliminate wrath; wrath is still stored up against the unrepentant. But grace does eliminate the necessity for everyone to experience it. Wise is the man or woman who takes God's grace.

8 SALVATION IN THE OLD TESTAMENT

It should be evident from comments made in the preceding study of the law that a person was saved under the Old Testament dispensation in the same way in which a person is saved today. That is, the person who lived before Christ's time was saved by grace through faith in the promise of a coming redeemer, just as today a person is saved by grace through faith in the redeemer who has already come. The Old Testament women and men looked forward to Christ. We look back. Beyond that, the grounds of salvation are identical. The Old Testament sacrifices pointed forward to Christ.

However, if an average Christian (not to mention a non-Christian) were asked how any one of the Old Testament figures was saved, it is likely that a wrong answer would be given. For example, some think that the old Testament figures were saved by being Jews. They base this view upon their understanding that God's promises to Israel were given to Israel collectively, that is, as including each and every descendant of Abraham. They would find support in such texts as John 4:22, in which Jesus told the woman of Samaria, "Salvation is from the Jews." That view was shared by the majority of Jews in Paul's day, as evidenced by his treatment of the subject in Romans 9. It is shared by most Jews and even by a significant number of Christians today. But are all Jews saved? Or to put it in a more limited way, were all Jews saved before Christ's day? Both the Old and the New Testaments deny that.

A second erroneous view, perhaps more common, is that the Old Testament figures were saved by keeping the law. That, of course, does not explain how Adam and Eve or Abraham and Sarah or any others who lived before the giving of the law were saved, but it does fit in with the fundamental human desire to achieve one's own salvation. Men and women earnestly want to be saved by doing something for themselves. Actually, the law condemns them.

Finally, some would say that the Old Testament figures were saved by keeping the sacraments, that is, by performing the sacrifices and other rites specified in the Levitical code. That gets closer to the real issue, for salvation did consist in what the sacrifices signified. Still, salvation was not by the sacrifices any more than it is by baptism or the Lord's Supper today.

To Whom He Chooses

How were the Old Testament figures saved? The apostle Paul was faced by those who thought that Jews were saved by birth, keeping the law, observing the sacrifices, or by some combination of the three. He answered such views by teaching that salvation is always by grace, not through works of any kind; hence salvation is always ultimately a matter of God's sovereign choice or election.

In Romans 4 Paul devotes an entire chapter to showing that Abraham, the father of the Jewish nation, was saved by faith apart from the law. But even if this does show God's way of salvation, it leaves unanswered the question why Israel as a whole was not responding to God's offer in Christ. Israel had received promises of Christ's coming and had the sacrifices, which pointed forward to him. Israel should have believed. Yet when the early preachers of the gospel went forth with their message, it seemed that Israel was largely rejecting the Savior, while the Gentiles by contrast were believing. Why? Was God casting off his people? Had the way of salvation changed? Paul answers such questions in chapter 9, first by denying that Jews were ever saved by birth. Always, he shows, some were not saved and others were. "For," he says, speaking spiritually, "not all who are descended from Israel belong to Israel, and not all are children of Abraham [that is, spiritual children] because they are his descendants" (Rom. 9:6-7). Second, he shows that those who are Abraham's true spiritual seed become so only by God's sovereign election. "It is not the children of the flesh who are the children of God, but the children of the promise" (Rom. 9:8). Therefore, Jews were saved during the Old Testament period and are saved today precisely as Gentiles are saved, that is, by God's electing grace focused in the work of Christ on Calvary.

What was Abraham when God called him? He was not a Jew in the later nationalistic sense, although he was to become the first of the Jewish nation. When God called Abraham, he was merely one member of a very large number of Semitic people who occupied the ancient Near East at that time, most of whom worshiped idols. Abraham himself came from such a family. Thus, he was saved, not because of any supposed merit in him (as if he had sought God, for he had not), but because God elected him to salvation.

God's election of Abraham is stated at several places in the Bible. Joshua, for example, delivered a final charge to the people in which he reminded them of their pagan past, God's deliverance of them from that past and their resulting obligation to serve him. At one point he deals with Abraham saying:

> Thus says the LORD, the God of Israel, "Your fathers lived of old beyond the Euphrates, Terah, the father of Abraham and of Nahor;

and they served other gods. Then I took your father Abraham from beyond the River and led him through all the land of Canaan, and made his offspring many. I gave him Isaac; and to Isaac I gave Jacob and Esau. And I gave Esau the hill country of Seir to possess, but Jacob and his children went down to Egypt. And I sent Moses and Aaron, and I plagued Egypt with what I did in the midst of it; and afterwards I brought you out."... Now therefore fear the LORD, and serve him in sincerity and in faithfulness; put away the gods which your fathers served beyond the River, and in Egypt, and serve the LORD. (Josh. 24:2-5, 14)

Those verses say clearly that Abraham was chosen by God from out of a pagan ancestry and that he, Terah and Nahor once worshiped false gods.

Isaiah says the same thing. "Hearken to me, you who pursue deliverance, you who seek the LORD; look to the rock from which you were hewn, and to the quarry from which you were digged. Look to Abraham your father and to Sarah who bore you" (Is. 51:1-2). Nothing in their ancestry could possibly commend Israel to God. Salvation is always of grace.

At other points in Paul's writing, he denies that Abraham was saved either by keeping the law or observing the sacraments. He shows that Abraham lived four hundred and thirty years before the law was even given (Gal. 3:17), and that he was declared righteous by God through faith before receiving the rite of circumcision (Rom. 4:9-11).

One might argue that although God's call of Abraham was according to grace ("After all, God had to start somewhere"), after that salvation was by physical descent. One might conclude that all Abraham's descendants were therefore saved. But that is precisely the opinion against which Paul writes in Romans and which he answers specifically in the ninth chapter. The Jews of Paul's day were arguing that they had a special relationship with God because of their physical descent from Abraham, but in doing so they had overlooked the fact that Abraham had more than one son. There had been Isaac, the child of God's promise. But before Isaac there had been Ishmael. What about Ishmael? Clearly God had chosen Isaac rather than Ishmael, though Isaac was younger, thereby demonstrating that salvation is the result of God's free choice and that (whatever we may think of the matter) he obviously does not grant the same privileges to everyone.

There were undoubtedly some who argued that the case of Isaac did not prove Paul's position. Isaac had been born of Abraham and Sarah, thus of two good Jewish parents, but Ishmael had been born of Abraham and Hagar, Sarah's Egyptian slave girl. Ishmael was of mixed blood, they would hold; so Paul's denial of salvation by birth was unproven. Paul answers by passing on to the next generation. In that generation, in the case of Isaac's two sons, Jacob and Esau, God made his choice between sons of the same Jewish mother. Moreover, lest anyone try to introduce the matter of age as a factor, the two boys are twins. And no one can argue that the choice was made on the basis of the character or moral choices of the sons; God announced his decision while the children were still in Rebecca's womb, that is, before either had a chance to do or choose anything. Paul writes of that generation: "When Rebecca had conceived children by one man, our forefather Isaac, though they were not yet born and had done nothing either good or bad, in order that God's purpose of election might continue, not because of works but because of his call, she was told, 'The elder will serve the younger.' As it is written, 'Jacob I loved, but Esau I hated' " (Rom. 9:10-13).

The point of the argument is that the choice of who would receive the blessing of salvation lay with God entirely, then as now. God gives life to whom he chooses.

Looking Ahead to the Redeemer

To say that the Jews of the Old Testament period were saved by the electing grace of God, as Gentiles are saved today, is only one part of the picture, however. Although election is the initiating cause of salvation, it is nevertheless only that. We are left with the questions: On what grounds does God save the ungodly? How can God forgive sin? Can God justify the ungodly and still be just? The importance of these questions leads to the importance of Christ's death even for the Old Testament figures.

The apostle Paul deals with this issue in at least two places. In his first full statement of the gospel, Paul speaks of the revelation of the righteousness of God through Christ. First, righteousness is "unto all and upon all them that believe" (Rom. 3:22 KJV). The words convey the idea of being clothed with that righteousness or else having it deposited to our account, as in a bank.

Second, Paul's argument is that God is shown to be righteous by the death of Christ. Before the time of Christ, God had been saving numerous Old Testament figures by election. But they were still sinners, so it appeared as if God were simply forgetting about their sin, which was not right. We may sympathize with God's decision to forgive, but that does not make it right. What about justice? What about the sin? Those questions are resolved by the revelation of God's righteousness in Jesus Christ. It was on the basis of Christ's death that God had been forgiving sin all along, though that death had not yet occurred. When it occurred, the mystery was explained—and God was seen to be just.

Paul expresses this by writing about those who had been "justified by his grace as a gift, through the redemption which is in Christ Jesus, whom God put forward as an expiation [better, *propitiation*] by his blood, to be received by faith. This was to show God's righteousness, because in his divine forbearance he had passed over former sins; it was to prove at the present time that he himself is righteous and that he justifies him who has faith in Jesus" (Rom. 3:24-26). The initiating cause in salvation is God's free grace but the formal cause is, and has always been, the death of the mediator.

The second important passage from Paul's writing on these themes is Galatians 3, in which Paul bases on Abraham his argument for salvation by grace through faith in the Lord Jesus Christ. There Paul says three things: Abraham was saved by believing God (Gal. 3:6); the essence of his belief was that God was going to send a Savior, who was Jesus Christ (3: 16); and the work of Christ was to be a work of redemption (3: 13-14).

Some may say, "Do you really mean that the Old Testament figures looked forward to Christ's coming and were saved by faith in him just as we look back to Christ and are saved by believing in him as our Savior? How could they believe in him? He had not yet come. The prophecies of his coming were vague. And if even Christ's disciples had a wrong idea of his ministry—thinking he was to be a political Messiah (Acts 1:6) —how could ordinary people have a correct view? How could anyone really be saved through faith in a coming redeemer?"

One answer is that many obviously did not look forward to Christ and so were not saved. Certainly, of the many who actually encountered Christ later on, most were not saved. The masses could be attracted by his teaching one day and praise him, but cry out for his crucifixion the next. In Christ's day, as in every period of Old Testament history, those who were saved were a remnant.

A second answer is that there were obviously different degrees of understanding. The essence of faith in all who had any understanding was that they recognized themselves to be sinners in need and turned to God for salvation. Each one who came honestly to present a sacrifice for sin confessed that much.

A full answer to the question goes beyond either of these, however. We must say on the basis of the fullest biblical evidence that many did believe. Further they undoubtedly understood more than we often give them credit for.

We find the evidence throughout the Scriptures. When

Adam and Eve sinned in Eden, God came to them to convict them of sin and lead them to repentance. When he clothed them with skins taken from animals he himself had undoubtedly slain, he already pictured the future death of Christ who would be slain by the Father in order that we who are sinners might be clothed with his righteousness. God promised a redeemer, saying to Satan, "I will put enmity between you and the woman, and between your seed and her seed; he shall bruise your head, and you shall bruise his heel" (Gen. 3:15). Clearly, these words do not refer simply to a general human fear of snakes, as some modern theologians would interpret them, but rather to the coming of the Messiah who would defeat Satan and destroy his power. That is where salvation from the curse of sin was to lie. That is what Adam and Eve understood. When their first child was born, they called him Cain, which means "here he is" or "Acquisition," thereby testifying to their faith (however mistaken) that the promised one had now come.

We have already looked at Abraham with reference to his election by God to salvation and his own personal faith in the redeemer who was to come. But we have not looked at what is probably the most important verse on the subject. In John 8:56, Jesus says, "Your father Abraham rejoiced that he was to see my day; he saw it and was glad."

One way of interpreting that difficult verse is to assume that Jesus meant that Abraham was alive in heaven (or Paradise) at the time, rejoicing in Christ's ministry. The difficulty with such a view is that the subject of dispute in John 8 is not Abraham's continued consciousness beyond the grave but rather Christ's pre-existence. Verse 58 says, "Before Abraham was, I am." If Christ had wanted to say that Abraham was still living and rejoiced in Christ's birth and ministry, it would have been more natural to use present tenses for the verbs ("Abraham is rejoicing to see my day; he sees it, and is glad"). It seems proper to refer the saying to Abraham's understanding in his own day rather than to something contemporary with Christ's ministry.

To place the vision in Abraham's time does not in itself solve the problem. For most of the rabbis did this—that is, they spoke of a vision of the Messiah which Abraham was supposed to have had—yet disagreed on how it happened.

Abraham's vision of Christ's day may well be found in the story of the near sacrifice of Isaac on Mt. Moriah. Here Abraham learned in a new way that "the Lord will provide." God came to Abraham and told him to take his son, the heir of the promise, and sacrifice him on a mountain three days' journey away. It must have been a terrible struggle for Abraham as he wrestled with God's command. He knew that he must obey God, but he also knew that God was a God of his word and that he had committed himself to produce a nation through Isaac. Isaac had no children at this point. So if God was telling Abraham to kill Isaac, then the God who had done a miracle in Isaac's birth would have to do a miracle in his death. There would have to be a resurrection.

The narrative indicates that Abraham expected to bring Isaac back down the mountain with him after the sacrifice (Gen. 22:5). And the author of Hebrews states explicitly, "By faith Abraham, when he was tested, offered up Isaac, and he who had received the promises was ready to offer up his only son, of whom it was said, 'Through Isaac shall your descendants be named.' He considered that God was able to raise men even from the dead; hence, figuratively speaking, he did receive him back" (Heb. 11:17-19).

Abraham believed that God was going to do a miracle in bringing Isaac back from the dead, precisely the miracle that God the Father did with Jesus Christ the Son, as the special language of those verses from Hebrews indicates. But even this is not all. For when the trial was over and God had intervened to save Isaac and provide a ram for the sacrifice in place of the boy, Abraham rejoiced and called the name of the place

Jehovah-jireh, which means "The LORD will provide" (Gen. 22:14). Earlier this could have meant, "The Lord will provide a resurrection of Isaac." Now it could only mean that the same God who provided a ram in substitution for Isaac would one day provide his own Son as the perfect substitute and sacrifice for our salvation. Thus Abraham saw the coming of Jesus, including the meaning of his death and resurrection and rejoiced in that coming.

Suppose we should ask Abraham, "Abraham, why are you in heaven today? Was it because you left your home in Ur of the Chaldees and went to Canaan? Was it because of your faith or your character or your obedience?"

"No," Abraham would say. "Haven't you read my story? God promised me a great inheritance. I believed his promises about it. And the greatest promise was that he would send a Savior through my line through whom he would bring blessing to all nations. I am in heaven because I believed that God would do that."

"How about you, Jacob? Why are you in heaven? Are you in heaven because of your faith or because you were born in the line of your grandfather Abraham?"

"No," Jacob answers. "I am in heaven because I looked for a redeemer. Remember how I spoke about him to my son Judah as I lay dying? I didn't know his name then. But I said, 'The scepter shall not depart from Judah, nor the ruler's staff from between his feet, until he comes to whom it belongs; and to him shall be the obedience of the peoples' (Gen. 49:10). I am in heaven because I looked for his coming."

"Why are you in heaven, David? It must be because of your character. You were called 'a man after God's own heart.' "

"My character!" says David. "Are you forgetting that I committed adultery with Bathsheba and then tried to cover it up by having her husband killed? I am in heaven because I looked for the one who was promised as my redeemer and the redeemer of my people. I knew that God had promised him a kingdom that would endure forever."

What about you, Isaiah? Did you expect the redeemer?" "Of course, I did," Isaiah answers. "I spoke of him as the one who 'has borne our griefs, and carried our sorrows,' who was 'wounded for our transgressions' and 'bruised for our iniquities.' I knew that the Lord would lay on him the iniquity of us all."

We come to the time of Christ and find the same kind of response, only now those who believe are not from the so-called important levels of society, from the palace of Herod or from among the priests. They are common people. They are people like Simeon to whom "it had been revealed . . . by the Holy Spirit that he should not see death before he had seen the Lord's Christ" (Lk. 2:26), or Anna, a prophetess, who when Simeon was blessing the infant Christ, "gave thanks to God, and spoke of him to all who were looking for the redemption of Jerusalem" (Lk. 2:38). Such has always been the faith of God's children. In announcing the birth of Christ the angel said, "You shall call his name Jesus, for he will save his people from their sins" (Mt. 1:21). In every age God has always had those who looked to that Savior for their salvation. In ancient times there were Abraham, Jacob, David, Isaiah, Malachi, and many more, both women and men. In Christ's time there were Elizabeth, Zechariah, John the Baptist, Joseph, Mary and many others. There are many today.

There is only one way of salvation. "For there is one God, and there is one mediator between God and men, the man Christ Jesus, who gave himself as a ransom for all, the testimony to which was borne at the proper time" (1 Tim. 2:5-6). It is to the person and work of this mediator that we must turn in the following chapters.

PART III
THE PERSON OF CHRIST

*In the beginning was the Word, and the Word
was with God, and the Word was God.
He was in the beginning with God.
(Jn. 1:1-2)*

*And the Word became flesh and
dwelt among us, full of grace and truth.
(Jn. 1:14)*

*For there is one God, and there is one
mediator between God and men, the
man Christ Jesus, who gave himself as a
ransom for all, the testimony to
which was borne at the proper time.
(1 Tim. 2:5-6)*

9

THE DEITY OF JESUS CHRIST

If you have been following the thoughts of the preceding chapters but are not yet a Christian, perhaps you are thinking we have placed all our eggs in too fragile a basket. We have obviously placed our entire hope for salvation from our own and this world's ills upon the shoulders of a promised redeemer, whom Christians identify as Jesus Christ of Nazareth. You may be wondering if any one person, however extraordinary, is equal to that task. How could any one man, a mere man, do so much?

That is the issue. Is it a man whom we are talking about? Or is he God? Christians readily admit that if Jesus were no more than a man, however remarkable he might be, he clearly could not be our Savior, nor is it likely that he did the many supernatural things attributed to him. On the other hand, if he is not only a man but is also God, then nothing is impossible to him and he did achieve our salvation. God cannot lie, so what he has promised he will necessarily perform. The question of Christ's deity is, therefore, *the* question about Jesus Christ.

The question does not mean that Jesus must be approached in some mystical way. On the contrary, we must approach him as a true man within the context of history, a man who actually said and did certain things. But we will not understand him even in that context until we recognize that he is also God and that his divinity alone gives meaning to his speech and actions.

That was the experience of the first disciples and apostles. Brunner writes that "only when they understand him as this absolute Lord, to whom the full divine sovereignty belongs, did Easter as victory, and Good Friday as a saving Fact, become intelligible. Only when they knew Jesus as the present Heavenly Lord, did they know themselves to be sharers in the Messianic Kingdom as men of the new, the Messianic era."[1] In considering the person of Jesus Christ we therefore want to begin with the teaching of those men, that is, with the Bible's own teaching.

Our Great God and Savior

We begin with the writings of the apostle Paul for, aside from Jesus himself, Paul was unquestionably the major teacher and theologian of the early church. Moreover, Paul was not one of Christ's original disciples, whose opinion we might suspect to be colored by personal affection. Rather Paul began as an enemy of Christ and the church, which in his youth he even tried to destroy. Further his was a carefully thought-out opposition. Paul, a serious-minded and pious Jew, approached religion on the premise of the unity of God. He was a monotheist. He thought that the Christians' claims to divinity for Jesus were nothing short of blasphemy. Clearly, if such a man as Paul was converted, it must have been on the grounds of a profound religious experience and sound evidence.

A key passage in which Paul reveals his understanding of Jesus is Philippians 2:5-11. In that brief section Paul traces Christ's life from eternity past, when he was in the form of God and equal to God, through the events of his earthly life to eternity future, where he once again is glorified with the Father. It has been described as a parabola, for it begins in an infinite past, descends to the point of Christ's death on the cross, and then ascends to an infinite future again.

> *Have this mind among yourselves, which is yours in Christ Jesus, who, though he was in the form of God, did not count equality with God a thing to be grasped, but emptied himself, taking the form of a servant, being born in the likeness of men. And being found in human form he humbled himself and became obedient unto death, even death on a cross. Therefore God has highly exalted him and bestowed on him the name which is above every name, that at the name of Jesus every knee should bow, in heaven and on earth and under the earth, and every tongue confess that Jesus Christ is Lord, to the glory of God the Father.*

In speaking of the position that Jesus enjoyed with the Father in eternity past, Paul uses two words that deserve close study. The first is the Greek word *morphē*, found in the phrase "the form of God." In English the word *form* usually refers to the outward shape of an object, that is, to something external. In the Bible that is one meaning—it occurs in Paul's description of those who have "a form of religion" but deny the power of it (2 Tim. 3:5)—but it is a less common meaning. Another use of the English word suggests the dominant biblical idea. Sometimes we say, "I'm in good form today," by which we mean not merely external appearance but internal fitness as well. That is what Paul has in mind primarily as he writes about Jesus in his preincarnate state. He means, as one commentator has phrased it, that "he possessed inwardly and displayed outwardly the very nature of God himself."[2]

The second word is even more important. It is *isos*, meaning "equal." We have it in English in the scientific terms "isomer," "isomorph," "isometric," and in "isosceles triangle." An isomer is a molecule having a slightly different structure from another molecule (as, for example, being a mirror image of it), but identical to it in chemical composition. An isomorph is something that has the same form as something else. Isometric means "in equal measure." An isosceles triangle has two equal sides. Paul's use of this word in reference to Jesus teaches that Jesus is God's equal.

Moreover, that is the way the passage moves as a whole. Having described how Jesus laid aside his former glory in order to become man and die for us, Paul goes on to show how he received that glory back, noting that he is now to be confessed as Lord by every intelligent creature in God's universe. In the last section "the name which is above every name" is the name of God, "the Lord." No other name than Lord can rightly be called "the name which is above every name." The passage flows on to his confession, for that is what the affirmation "Jesus is Lord" means. It means "Jesus is God." Paul's phrasing of the homage of the universe to Jesus is a fairly direct allusion to Isaiah 45:23, in which God declares that he himself will be the object of universal adoration: "To me every knee shall bow, every tongue shall swear."

These verses in Philippians are remarkable for their high theology where the Lord Jesus Christ is concerned. They cut across all lesser confessions of Christ's person, showing that any view that would make him merely a great teacher or a great prophet is inadequate. They are also remarkable because their doctrine of Christ is indirect. That is, it is brought forward, not for its own sake, but in support of another point entirely. Paul's major point is not that Jesus is who he is but rather that we should be like him. An English commentator has written of this section of Paul's letter:

We have here a chain of assertions about our Lord Jesus Christ, made within some thirty years of his death at Jerusalem; made in the open day of public Christian intercourse, and made (every reader must feel this) not in the least manner of controversy, of assertion against difficulties and denials, but in the tone of a settled, common, and most living certainty. These assertions give us on the one hand the fullest possible assurance that he is man, man in nature, in circumstances and experience, and particularly in the sphere of relation to God the Father. But they also assure us, in precisely the same tone, and in a way which is equally vital to the argument in hand, that he is as genuinely divine as he is genuinely human.[3]

The various parts of Paul's doctrine of the Lord Jesus Christ are stated in that passage with unusual fullness, and therefore we have looked at it at some length. But one must not conclude that the letter to the Philippians is the only place in which such high themes are presented. On the contrary, they occur in much the same way, though less elaborately developed, throughout Paul's writings.

Two passages with the same scope (from eternity past to eternity future) are 2 Corinthians 8:9 and Galatians 4:4. In the former, Paul speaks of the Lord Jesus Christ who "though . . . rich, yet for your sake he became poor" that we "by his poverty . . . might become rich." In the second passage he writes that "when the time had fully come, God sent forth his Son, born of woman, born under the law, to redeem those who were under the law, so that we might receive adoption as sons." In both cases Paul is thinking of a former glory of Christ temporarily laid aside in order that he might accomplish our redemption. All passages that speak of God "sending his own Son" are also in this framework (compare Rom. 8:3; 1 Cor. 15:47; Eph. 4:8-10). In Colossians 1:19 we are told that "in him all the fulness of God was pleased to dwell." In Colossians 2:9: "In him the whole fulness of deity dwells bodily." In other places Paul speaks of Jesus as God "manifested in the flesh" (1 Tim. 3:16), of his appearance on earth as an "epiphany" (2 Tim. 1:10, Greek text) and, most dramatic of all, of "our great God and Savior Jesus Christ" (Tit. 2:13).[4]

"The conception of the person of Christ which underlies and finds expression in the epistle to the Hebrews is indistinguishable from that which governs all the allusions to our Lord in the epistles of Paul,"[5] wrote B. B. Warfield, professor of theology at Princeton Theological Seminary until his death in 1921. Hebrews 2, like Philippians 2:5-11, is based on the premise of the pre-existence and full divinity of Christ. Its major point is that Christ moved from his prior position of glory to the Incarnation in order to achieve our salvation and is now fully glorified once again. "Thou didst make him for a little while lower than the angels, thou hast crowned him with glory and honor, putting everything in subjection under his feet" (2:7-8). "We see Jesus, who for a little while was made lower than the angels [that is, was made a man], crowned with glory and honor because of the suffering of death" (2:9). Elsewhere in Hebrews Jesus is described as reflecting "the glory of God" and bearing "the very stamp of his nature" (1:3), "holy, blameless, unstained, separated from sinners" (7:26), and one to whom shall be given "glory for ever and ever" (13:21).

The Word Made Flesh
In the books traditionally ascribed to the apostle John, particularly the fourth Gospel, the deity of Christ is the overriding theme. The purpose of Mark's Gospel, if it may be so narrowed down, is to reveal the Lord Jesus Christ as God's servant. Matthew portrays him as the Jewish Messiah. Luke stresses Christ's humanity. But in John, Jesus is revealed as the eternal, pre-existing Son of God, who became man in order to reveal the Father and bring eternal life through his death and resurrection. In fact, toward the end of the Gospel, John tells us explicitly that this is his purpose: "Now Jesus did many other signs in the presence of the disciples, which are not written in this book; but these are written that you may believe that Jesus is the Christ, the Son of God, and that believing you may have life in his name" (Jn. 20:30-31).

Since that is John's purpose in writing, we are not surprised to find this great thesis—Jesus is God—at the very beginning. There he writes: "In the beginning was the Word, and the Word was with God, and the Word was God. He was in the beginning with God" (1:1-2). We know from verse 14, which says that "the Word became flesh," that this key term, *Word,* refers to Jesus. Hence, the opening verses of the Gospel are telling us that Jesus was with God from the very beginning, that is, from eternity past, and was in fact himself fully God. The opening sentences of the Gospel are a categorical statement of Christ's divinity. There are three distinct statements in these verses, one of them being repeated again in slightly different language.

The first statement, the one repeated, is that Jesus existed with God "in the beginning." This phrase is used in several different ways in the Bible. In 1 John it is used of the beginning of Christ's earthly ministry: "That which was from the beginning, which we have heard, which we have seen with our eyes, which we have looked upon and touched with our hands, concerning the word of life . . . we proclaim also to you" (1 Jn. 1:1-3). In Genesis it is used of the beginning of creation: "In the beginning God created the heavens and the earth" (Gen. 1:1). But in John's Gospel the reference in the phrase goes back even beyond that. John is referring to eternity past, saying in effect that when a person begins to talk about Jesus Christ he or she can do so properly only by going back beyond his earthly life, beyond even the beginning of creation, into eternity. That is where Jesus was. In that perspective John is clearly at one with the teaching of Paul in Philippians and with the teaching of the book of Hebrews.

The second statement in John 1 is that Jesus Christ was "with" God. This is an affirmation of Christ's separate personality in the sense that it has come to be expressed in the doctrine of the division of persons within the Trinity. But it is subtle. John wishes to say that Jesus is fully God. Later he will report Jesus as saying, "He who has seen me has seen the Father" (Jn. 14:9). But John is also aware that there is diversity within the Godhead, and he expresses that by this statement.

The final statement is the declaration that Jesus is fully

divine. The Greek text says literally, "And God was the Word," which means "And fully divine in all respects was Jesus." Everything that can be said about the Father can be said of the Son as well. Is the Father sovereign? So is Jesus. Is the Father omniscient? So is Jesus. Is he omnipresent? So is Jesus. In fact, in Jesus may be found all the wisdom, glory, power, love, holiness, justice, goodness and truth of God.

In a sense, everything that follows in John's Gospel illustrates that Jesus is God. John organizes the Gospel as a student might organize a term paper, first telling what he is going to prove, then proving it, and finally summarizing it as if to say to the reader, "See, I have done what I said I would do." Because of that, everything in the Gospel could be considered at this point of our study: the miracles, the discourses, the reaction of Christ's enemies and friends, even John's own comments.

Instead of doing that in full, however, it may be worth taking a single text as indicative of John's overall orientation. This text shows without question that John's conception of Christ was the highest that can possibly be imagined. The text is John 12:41, in which after John has referred to Isaiah's vision of God (Is. 6), he says, "Isaiah said this because he saw his [Jesus'] glory and spoke of him."

To people living today, particularly Christians, the reference may seem natural, for we are used to theological statements giving full deity to Christ. But that was hardly natural for John, a monotheistic Jew, or for his contemporaries. For a Jew of John's time God was almost inaccessible in his transcendence. He was the holy One of Israel. He dwelt in glory unapproachable. None actually saw him. And when on some unusual occasion some remarkably privileged person, such as Moses or Isaiah, had received a vision of God in his glory, it was not believed even then to be an actual vision of God as he is in himself but rather only an image or reflection of him. Yet such a vision filled one with awe and wonder.

What Isaiah saw was the closest thing in all Jewish writings or tradition to an actual "portrait" of the living and holy God. Yet that vision with all its breathtaking splendor John applies to Jesus. Without questioning, it would seem, John takes the most exalted vision of God in the Old Testament and says that it was a portrait of a carpenter from Nazareth who was about to be crucified—so great is John's opinion of him.

I Am: Christ's Claims

Where did these men, who were obviously impressed with Christ but who were not fools, get such an opinion of him? Why did they believe that he is God? The answer to those questions is on two levels. First, because that is what Jesus himself taught. Second, because their observation of his life left no other explanation.

Christ's own claims occur throughout the Gospels, both directly and indirectly. Practically everything Jesus said was an indirect claim to divinity. His first preaching is an example. When John the Baptist had come declaring the imminent arrival of God's kingdom, he pointed to one who would himself embody that kingdom. When Jesus came, his own first preaching was an announcement of the kingdom's arrival. "The time is fulfilled, and the kingdom of God is at hand; repent, and believe in the gospel" (Mk. 1:15). Later he said of himself in speaking to the Pharisees, "The kingdom of God is in the midst of you" (Lk. 17:21). He was claiming that the prophecies of the Old Testament were about him and were fulfilled in him.

All Christ's words about the Old Testament fall into that category. The sum of his teaching was "Think not that I have come to abolish the law and the prophets; I have come not to abolish them but to fulfil them" (Mt. 5:17). When he invited men to follow him—"Follow me, and I will make you fishers of men" (Mt. 4:19)—he implied that he was of sufficient stature to be worth following. When he forgave sins, he did it knowing he was doing what only God can do (Mk. 2:1-12). Toward the end of his life he promised to send God's Holy Spirit to be with the disciples after his departure, which again implies divinity.

Very remarkable among his claims was his unique reference to God as his Father. That was by no means a common form of expression in Judaism (as it is in the English language). No Jew ever spoke of God directly as "my Father." Yet that was the form of address Jesus used, particularly in his prayers. In fact, it was his only mode of addressing God. It referred to his relationship to the Father exclusively. Jesus said, "I and the Father are one" (Jn. 10:30). He said, "Father, the hour has come; glorify thy Son that the Son may glorify thee.... O righteous Father, the world has not known thee, but I have known thee" (Jn. 17:1, 25). Eventually he taught his disciples to address God as Father also, as a result of their relationship to himself. But even in that case his relationship to God as Father and their relationship to God as Father were different. Thus he spoke to Mary Magdalene saying, "Go to my brethren and say to them, I am ascending to my Father and your Father, to my God and your God" (Jn. 20:17). He did not say "to *our* Father" or "to *our* God." "So close was his connection with God that he equated a man's attitude to himself with his attitude to God. Thus, to know him was to know God (Jn. 8:19, 14:7); to see him was to see God (Jn. 12:45, 14:9); to believe in him was to believe in God (Jn. 12:44, 14:1); to receive him was to receive God (Mk. 9:37); to hate him was to hate God (Jn. 15:23); and to honor him was to honor God (Jn. 5:23)."[6]

Jesus' "I am" sayings are worthy of special notice, for he claimed to be all that human beings need for a full spiritual life. Only God can rightly make such claims. "I am the bread of life" (Jn. 6:35). "I am the light of the world" (Jn. 8:12; 9:5). "I am the door" (Jn. 10:7, 9). "I am the good shepherd" (Jn. 10:11, 14). "I am the resurrection and the life" (Jn. 11:25). "I am the way, and the truth, and the life" (Jn. 14:6). "I am the true vine" (Jn. 15:1, 5).

In addition to these indirect statements, a number of statements claim divinity directly. Such claims were considered blasphemous in Christ's day and were punishable by death. To avoid a hasty and premature death, Jesus had to be careful in what he said and to whom. Nevertheless, he made a number of direct claims. In John 8, for example, the leaders of the people had been challenging everything Jesus said and now challenged his statement that Abraham had rejoiced that he was to see the day of Christ and had seen it and was glad. They said, "You are not yet fifty years old, and have you seen Abraham?" He replied, using his most solemn form of introducing a saying, "Truly, truly, I say to you, before Abraham was, I am" (Jn. 8:57-58). That so infuriated the leaders that they immediately took up stones to stone him.

To our way of thinking it is a bit hard to see why that particular saying would have provoked such a violent response. Stoning was the penalty for blasphemy, for making oneself out to be God. But how does one get blasphemy from Jesus' words? It is obvious from the saying itself that Jesus was claiming to have existed before Abraham was born. It is also obvious from the tense of the verb—"before Abraham was, I *am*" —that he was claiming an eternal pre-existence. But that alone would not be sufficient cause for stoning. The real reason for their violent reaction is that when Jesus said "I am," he was using the divine name by which God had revealed himself to Moses at the burning bush. When Moses had asked, "If I come to the people of Israel and say to them, 'The God of your fathers has sent me to you,' and they ask me, 'What is his name?' what shall I say to them?" God said to Moses, "I AM WHO I AM. . . . Say this to the people of Israel, 'I AM has sent me to you' " (Ex. 3:13-14). That is the name that Jesus took to himself. Because of that, the Jews, who immediately recognized his claim for what it was, reached out to kill him.

A final example of Christ's unique conception of himself occurred shortly after the resurrection on the day that Jesus appeared among the disciples, Thomas being present. Jesus had appeared to the disciples earlier when Thomas was absent. But when Thomas was told about the appearance, Thomas had replied, "Unless I see in his hands the print of the nails, and place my finger in the mark of the nails, and place my hand in his side, I will not believe" (Jn. 20:25). Then the Lord appeared to them once more and asked Thomas to make the test he had wanted to make. "Put your finger here, and see my hands; and put out your hand, and place it in my side" (20:27). Overcome by Christ's presence, Thomas immediately fell to the ground and worshiped him, saying, "My Lord and my God!" (20:28). Lord and God! *Adonai! Elohim!* And Jesus accepted that designation. He did not deny it.

Good Man, Madman, Con Man or Son of Man?

We have traced the claims of Christ's divinity through the writings of the apostle Paul, the book of Hebrews and John's Gospel to the teachings of Jesus himself. "Is it possible to believe this?" someone might ask. "But is it possible to believe that a carpenter from Nazareth, however extraordinary, was actually God?" Well, what are the possibilities?

One truly impossible answer was first given by the people of Jerusalem. They said on one occasion, "He is a good man" (Jn. 7:12). Whatever else he may be, he certainly cannot be merely a good man. No man can honestly make the claims he made. He put himself forward as the Savior of the human race, claiming to be God and therefore being able to save. Is he? If so, he is obviously much more than a man. If not, then he is at best mistaken (consequently, not "good") and at worst a deceiver. What are we to do with his claims? We cannot escape them. "The claims are there. They do not in themselves constitute evidence of deity. The claims may have been false. But some explanation of them must be found. We cannot any longer regard Jesus as simply a great Teacher, if he was so grievously mistaken in one of the chief subjects of his teaching, namely himself."[7] Similarly, "You must make your choice. Either this man was, and is, the Son of God: or else a madman or something worse. You can shut him up for a fool, you can spit at him and kill him for a demon; or you can fall at his feet and call him Lord and God. But let us not come with any patronising nonsense about his being a great human teacher. He has not left that open to us. He did not intend to."[8]

The one impossible explanation of the person of Christ is, then, that he was a good man, a good and outstanding teacher to whom we should listen and from whom we should all learn. The quotation from C. S. Lewis has already suggested the remaining possibilities. There are three of them.

First, Jesus may have been *mad*. Or he was suffering from megalomania. That was the view of some in his own day who said, "You have a demon" (Jn. 7:20). Hitler suffered from megalomania. So also, probably, did Napoleon. Perhaps Jesus was like them. Was he? Before we jump too quickly at that explanation we need to ask whether the total character of Jesus (as we know it) bears out this speculation. Did he act like one who was crazy? Did he speak like one suffering from megalomania? It is hard to read the Gospels and be satisfied with this explanation. Rather, as we read the Gospels the conclusion seems to be forced upon us that, rather than being mad, Jesus was actually the sanest man who ever lived. He spoke with quiet authority. He always seemed to be in control of the situation. He was never surprised or rattled. He will not fit that easy classification.

Charles Lamb is reported to have said, "If Shakespeare were to come into this room we should all rise up to meet him, but if that Person [he meant Jesus] were to come into it, we should all fall down and try to kiss the hem of his garment."

Another reason why Jesus could not have been crazy is the reaction of others to him. Men and women did not merely tolerate him; they either were for him or else were violently against him. That is not the way we react to those who are crazy. We may be irritated by a madman's irrational behavior. We may ignore him. We may lock him up if his delusions are dangerous. But we do not kill him. Yet that is what men who did not follow Jesus tried to do to him.

A second possibility is that Jesus was a *deceiver*, the view of some others (Jn. 7:12). That is, he deliberately set out to fool people. Before we settle on that answer, however, we need to be clear about what is involved in it. In the first place, if Jesus really was a deceiver he was certainly the best deceiver who ever lived. Jesus claimed to be God, but that claim was not made in a Greek or Roman environment where the idea of many gods or even half-gods was acceptable. It was made at the heart of monotheistic Judaism. The Jews were ridiculed, at times persecuted, for their strict belief in one God. Nevertheless they stuck to that doctrine and were fanatical in its defense. In that theological climate Christ made his claims—and what happened? The remarkable thing is that he got people to believe in him. Lots of people—men and women, peasants and sophisticates, priests, eventually even members of his own family.

On the other hand, if Jesus was a deceiver, if he was not God, he could be termed a devil. Think it through clearly. Jesus did not merely say "I am God" and let it go at that. He said, "I am God come to save fallen humanity; I am the means of salvation; trust me with your life and your future." Jesus taught that God is holy and that we are barred from him because we are not holy. Our sin is a barrier between ourselves and God. Moreover, he taught that he had come to do something about our problem. He would die for our sin; he would bear its punishment. All who would trust in him would be saved. That is good news, even great news—but only if it is true. If it is not true, then his followers are of all human beings the most miserable, and Jesus Christ should be hated as a fiend from hell. If it is not true, Jesus has sent generations of gullible followers to a hopeless eternity.

But is he a deceiver? Is that the only explanation we can give for one who was known for being "meek and lowly," who became a poor itinerant evangelist in order to help the poor and teach those whom others despised, who said, "Come to me, all who labor and are heavy laden, and I will give you rest" (Mt. 11:28)? Somehow the facts do not fit. We cannot face the facts of his life and teaching and still call this man a deceiver. What then? If he was not a deceiver and he was not mad, only one possibility is left. Jesus is who he said he is. He is God, and we should follow him.[9]

10 THE HUMANITY OF CHRIST

Although there are those today, as in every age, who deny Christ's divinity, there are also those who affirm his divinity but stop with that description of him. This is also an error. A second, equally important fact is that he is also fully man. He is not man from eternity past, as is true of his Godhead. He became man at a particular point in time through the Incarnation. Now, having become man, he is the God-man to whom alone we look for salvation.

In the Bible this truth is everywhere apparent, even in the Old Testament. For example, in that prophecy from Isaiah so often read at Christmastime, the twofold nature of the coming Christ is described. "For to us a child is born, to us a son is given; and the government will be upon his shoulder, and his name will be called 'Wonderful Counselor, Mighty God, Everlasting Father, Prince of Peace' " (Is. 9:6). Here two important verbs are used of Christ's coming: "is born" and "is given." As a child he is *born*, but as a Son he is *given*. The same distinction occurs in Paul's writings. Thus we read, "Concerning his

Son, who was descended from David according to the flesh and designated Son of God in power according to the Spirit of holiness by his resurrection from the dead, Jesus Christ our Lord" (Rom. 1:3-4). Jesus was descended from David according to the flesh, but he was also designated God's Son. We read, "But when the time had fully come, God sent forth his Son, born of woman, born under the law, to redeem those who were under the law, so that we might receive adoption as sons" (Gal. 4:4-5). As a Son, Jesus Christ was *sent,* because he was always God's Son. Nevertheless, he was *born* of woman under the law, and thus became man. The Bible is never hesitant to put the twin truths of the full deity and true humanity of the Lord Jesus Christ together.

These truths are also illustrated through various events in Christ's ministry. For instance, in the second chapter of John's Gospel the Lord is at a wedding (Jn. 2:1-11). Few things could be more human than that. Yet when the wine is exhausted and the host about to be embarrassed, Jesus makes new and better wine from the water in the great stone waterpots used for the Jewish purifications.

On another occasion the disciples were crossing the Sea of Galilee from Capernaum to the land of the Gadarenes. Jesus, exhausted from the day's activities, was asleep in the boat. A storm arose that was so intense it frightened even those seasoned fishermen. They awoke him saying, "Save, Lord; we are perishing," and Jesus stilled the storm. What could be more human than our Lord's total exhaustion in the boat? What could be more divine than his stilling of the winds and waves? The disciples exclaimed, "What sort of man is this, that even winds and sea obey him?" (Mt. 8:23-27).

Nothing could be more human than Jesus' death by crucifixion. Nothing could be more divine than the darkening of the sky, the tearing of the veil of the temple, the opening of the graves of the saints buried near Jerusalem, and the triumphant rending of the tomb on that first Easter morning.

Twin Truths; Twin Heresies

These twin truths have not always been acknowledged by everyone in all periods of church history. There is hardly a doctrine of Christianity that has not been denied by someone sometime. The heresy of denial of Christ's divinity usually goes by the name of Arianism (after Arius of Alexandria; died 335). Arius taught that the Son of God and the Holy Spirit were beings willed into existence by God for the purposes of redemption. Thus they were not eternal, as God is. There was a time "before which they were not."

The error on the other side, the heresy of denying Christ's true humanity, goes by the name of Docetism. Docetism grew out of a movement known as Gnosticism, which was more or less contemporary with the early years of Christianity. It had two major characteristics. First, there was a principle which one commentator calls "the supremacy of the intellect and the superiority of mental enlightenment to faith and conduct."[1] The Gnostics thought of themselves as "the knowing ones," which is what the word _gnostic_ means, believing that salvation is primarily by knowledge, that is, by initiation into the mystical and allegedly superior knowledge which they possessed. Of course in such a system, the literal Incarnation of the Son of God was meaningless. What was important was the "Christ-idea" or the truths that Christ announced.

A second characteristic of the Gnostic system was its belief in the radical and unbridgeable gulf between spirit and matter, coupled with the conviction that matter is inherently evil and spirit alone is good. This view was held in common by most other systems of thought in that period. On the one hand it led to a denial of the importance of the moral life; salvation was in the realm of the mind or spirit, which alone is good, and therefore what the body did could not matter. On the other hand it produced a type of philosophical religion that was divorced from concrete history. Obviously, Gnosticism came into conflict with authentic Christianity. Given its system, any real Incarnation of the Son of God was impossible. If matter is evil, then God could not have taken a human body upon himself. And if that is so, then the Incarnation of God in Christ must have been in appearance only. The word *Docetism* comes from the Greek verb *dokeō* which means "to appear." In some forms of supposedly Christian Gnosticism the Incarnation was therefore expressed by saying that the Spirit of God merely came upon the man Jesus at the time of his baptism, remained with him during the years of his ministry, and then deserted him just before his crucifixion. In other forms, it was said that Jesus only seemed to be a man, but actually was not one. Therefore, he did not really possess a material body, did not really die and so on.

Docetism was anathema to Christianity, of course, so it was forcefully rejected. The first written reply to such views is that of the apostle John, preserved in his Epistles primarily. He insists on the true Incarnation of the Son of God. Thus, his first Epistle begins by stressing the apostles' own physical experience of Jesus, "That which was from the beginning, which we have heard, which we have seen with our eyes, which we have looked upon and touched with our hands, concerning the word of life—the life was made manifest, and we saw it, and testify to it, and proclaim to you the eternal life which was with the Father and was made manifest to us—that which we have seen and heard we proclaim also to you, so that you may have fellowship with us" (1 Jn. 1:1-3). These verses refer to three of the five physical senses. Later John gives this test of true Christianity: "Every spirit which confesses that Jesus Christ has come in the flesh is of God, and every spirit which does not confess Jesus is not of God. This is the spirit of antichrist, of which you heard that it was coming, and now it is in the world already" (1 Jn. 4:2-3).

Sometime later, Marcion of Pontus, who taught in Rome about the middle of the second century, also popularized Docetist views. He is known mostly for his rejection of the Old

Testament as well as parts of the New. But he was also a threat to the church through his rejection of the materiality of Christ's body. Another early heresy was Manichaeanism which had a strong influence on Augustine's early years. It included the belief that Christ's body was composed of "heavenly" but not true material flesh. These errors were rejected soundly in a series of early church councils. The Creed of Chalcedon (A.D. 451) declares that the Lord Jesus Christ is

> _truly God and truly man, of a reasonable_ [_rational_] _soul and body; consubstantial_ [_coessential_] _with the Father according to the Godhead, and consubstantial with us according to the manhood; in all things like unto us without sin; begotten before all ages of the Father according to the Godhead, and in these latter days, for us and for our salvation, born of the Virgin Mary, the Mother of God, according to the manhood; one and the same Christ, Son, Lord, Only-begotten, to be acknowledged in two natures inconfusedly, unchangeably, indivisibly, inseparably; the distinction of natures being by no means taken away by the union, but rather the property of each nature being preserved, and concurring in one Person and one Subsistence, not parted or divided into two persons, but one and the same Son, Only-begotten, God, the Word, the Lord Jesus Christ._

The Athanasian Creed, attributed to Athanasius, a great third-century defender of orthodoxy, but more likely composed after Chalcedon, says more simply: "Our Lord Jesus Christ, the Son of God, is God and man ... perfect God, and perfect man ... who although he be [is] God and man; yet he is not two, but one Christ; one, not by conversion of the Godhead into flesh: but by taking [assumption] of the manhood into God." These creeds and the Scriptures they are based on teach that Jesus, the Son of God, became like us in every respect (except for sin) so that we might become like him.

Christ's Emotional Life

One area in which Jesus became like us through the Incarnation is the emotional life, as B. B. Warfield pointed out in an essay on that subject in the early years of this century.[2] Some in the church have wanted to separate Christ from all emotions, as if emotions are not quite appropriate to him. Others have exaggerated his emotions to the point at which he hardly commands our reverence. The true picture, as presented in the New Testament, is somewhat between the two.

The emotion most frequently attributed to Christ is *compassion* or *pity*. It is his expression of deep love when confronted by the desperate need of fallen men and women. Sometimes it is occasioned by physical need. Thus on one occasion, when confronted by the hunger of a large crowd that had been following him, Jesus said, "I have compassion on the crowd, because they have been with me now three days, and have nothing to eat; and if I send them away hungry to their homes, they will faint on the way; and some of them have come a long way" (Mk. 8:2-3). We are told that he was "moved with pity" at the sight of a leper, and healed him (Mk. 1:41), that he responded "in pity" to the appeal for healing by two blind men (Mt. 20:34), that "compassion" caused him to raise the dead son of the widow of Nain (Lk. 7:13). Spiritual need also drew forth his compassion. We are told again and again that he had compassion on the multitudes because "they were like sheep without a shepherd" (Mk. 6:34; see also Mt. 9:36; 14:14). At other times he actually wept aloud over the stubborn unbelief of the city of Jerusalem (Lk. 19:41) and at the tomb of Lazarus (Jn. 11:35).

Mention of Christ's tears leads to another area of Christ's emotional life, the area of *grief* leading even to *indignation* and *anger*. One important example of his grief, though difficult to interpret, is his weeping at the tomb of Lazarus. An unusual word, *enebrimēsatō*, is used either to say that Jesus was "angry" at what was taking place or else that he was "deeply moved." In the New Testament it is found in only three other passages (Mt. 9:30; Mk. 1:43; 14:5, in two of them meaning "sternly charged" and in the third "reproached." Neither of these meanings seems to fit the context of Christ's response at the tomb of Lazarus. However, William Barclay believes each of them seems to contain "a certain sternness, almost anger." Some commentators have placed the idea of indignation or even anger in John's passage. They would translate the verse, "Jesus was moved to anger in his spirit." If we ask why Jesus should be angry, they answer either that he was angry with the supposed unbelief or hypocrisy of those who were weeping over Lazarus or else he was angry with death, which he would have viewed as a tool of Satan and a great enemy. Insincerity is not mentioned or implied in the passage, however, and whatever may have been true of the crowd, Mary and Martha were certainly not faking their grief.

The other possibility, translating the word to suggest deep emotion, rests on the fact that one other known use of the word _enebrimēsatō_ in the Greek language is to describe the snorting of a horse, as in the excitement of battle or under a heavy load. Thus Jesus may be said to have groaned with the sisters in deep emotion, emotion out of which an involuntary cry was wrung from his heart. That is the view of J. B. Phillips, who rendered the phrase, "He was deeply moved and visibly distressed," and by the translators of the New International Version, who say, "He was deeply moved and troubled."

Some Christians have found this unacceptable, for they imagine that it is not proper for Jesus to have been moved to such a degree, particularly by the grief of others. But how can we read the passage without seeing that Jesus wept with the sisters in their grief? "The expression used . . . implies that he now voluntarily and deliberately accepts and makes his own the emotion and the experience from which it is his purpose to deliver men."[3] "He . . . gathered up into his own personality all the misery resulting from sin, represented in a dead man and broken-hearted people round him."[4]

At times, however, the grief displayed by Jesus went on to

anger, as in his stern denunciations of the religious leaders of his day. He calls them "hypocrites" (Mt. 15:7), "white-washed tombs" (Mt. 23:27), "serpents" (Mt. 23:33), "blind guides" (Mt. 15:14), and "of [their] father the devil" (Jn. 8:44). At times he could even be moved with anger against his own disciples. On the occasion when the disciples in a fit of self-importance tried to keep the children from coming to Jesus, we read, "But when Jesus saw it he was indignant, and said to them, 'Let the children come to me, do not hinder them; for to such belongs the kingdom of God' " (Mk. 10:14).

It is not an impassible, insensitive, unmovable Christ that is presented to us in the New Testament. Rather it is one who has entered into our griefs and understands our sorrows, one who was on occasion moved to righteous indignation and angered by sin.

A third area of Christ's emotional life is that of *joy* or *gladness*. Warfield writes:

We call our Lord "the Man of Sorrows," and the designation is obviously appropriate for one who came into the world to bear the sins of men and to give his life a ransom for many. It is, however, not a designation which is applied to Christ in the New Testament, and even in the Prophet (Isa. 53:3) it may very well refer rather to the objective afflictions of the righteous servant than to his subjective distresses. In any event we must bear in mind that our Lord did not come into the world to be broken by the power of sin and death, but to break it. He came as a conqueror with the gladness of the imminent victory in his heart; for the joy set before him he was able to endure the cross, despising the shame (Heb. 12:2). And as he did not prosecute his work in doubt of the issue, neither did he prosecute it hesitantly as to its methods. He rather (so we are told, Luke 10:21) "exulted in the Holy Spirit" as he contemplated the ways of God in bringing many sons to glory.[5]

Sometimes Jesus spoke of his own joy and of his desire that it also be possessed by his followers. "These things I have spoken to you, that my joy may be in you, and that your joy may be full" (Jn. 15:11). Again, in his high priestly prayer of John 17, "Now I am coming to thee; and these things I speak in the world, that they may have my joy fulfilled in themselves" (17:13).

Like Us in Temptation and Suffering

Two more areas in which Jesus clearly became like us by means of his Incarnation are important in relating to him as our guide in living the Christian life.

The first is that he became subject to _temptation_. "For we have not a high priest who is unable to sympathize with our weaknesses, but one who in every respect has been tempted as we are, yet without sin" (Heb. 4:15). We have a dramatic illustration of what this means in the story of Christ's temptation by Satan, recorded in Matthew 4:1-11 (parallel, Lk. 4:1-13). After his baptism by John, Jesus was driven into the wilderness to be tempted by the devil. He spent forty days in fasting and then the temptations began. The first was physical, the temptation to turn stones to bread. We learn the significance of it from Jesus' reply to Satan: "Man shall not live by bread alone, but by every word that proceeds from the mouth of God" (Mt. 4:4). It was the temptation to put physical needs over spiritual ones.

The second temptation was spiritual. The devil took Jesus to a pinnacle of the temple in Jerusalem and challenged him to throw himself down, presuming upon God to rescue him. The devil said, "If you are the Son of God, throw yourself down; for it is written, 'He will give his angels charge of you,' and 'On their hands they will bear you up, lest you strike your foot against a stone' " (4:6). Jesus answered that it would be wrong to do that because it is also written that we shall not put God to the test.

Finally, the devil produced a vocational temptation. He knew that Jesus was to receive the kingdoms of this world for his glory; it had been prophesied in the Old Testament. "Ask of me, and I will make the nations your heritage, and the ends of the earth your possession" (Ps. 2:8). But the way to that inheritance was the cross, and Satan now argued that Jesus could obtain it without suffering. He would help. He said, "All these I will give you, if you will fall down and worship me" (Mt. 4:9). Jesus rejected Satan's offer and instead set his face to go in the way that God had set before him.

A final area in which Jesus became like us in order that we might become like him is in *suffering*. Some of it was emotional and spiritual suffering. Some was physical. We read that Christ experienced hunger. That was true many times, no doubt, but we are told so explicitly in connection with his wilderness temptation (Mt. 4:2). He also experienced thirst. On one occasion, weary with his journey, he sat on Jacob's well and asked a woman of Samaria for a drink. On the cross he cried, "I thirst," and they gave him vinegar (Jn. 19:28-29). Once when he fell asleep in a wildly rocking boat, he was so tired that even the wind and waves failed to rouse him. The greatest example of his suffering was the anguish of soul and body endured on the cross, before which even his soul shrank (Lk. 22:39-46; compare Mt. 26:36-46, Mk. 14:32-42).

Jesus, by means of the Incarnation, came to know all the vicissitudes of life: trials, joys, sufferings, losses, gains, temptations, griefs. He entered into them, understood them, and thus became a pattern for us, that we should go through these experiences as he did, and also an encouragement to us to come to him in prayer, knowing that he understands what we are going through. Peter speaks of the value of Christ as a pattern when he encouraged those of his day to endure suffering as Christ did. "For to this you have been called, because Christ also suffered for you, leaving you an example, that you should follow in his steps" (1 Pet. 2:21). The author of Hebrews refers to our encouragement in prayer, saying, "For surely it is not with angels that he [Christ] is concerned but with the descendants of Abraham. Therefore he had to be made like his brethren in every respect, so that he might become a merciful and faithful high priest in the service of God, to make expiation for the sins of the people. For because he himself has suffered and been tempted, he is able to help those who are tempted" (Heb. 2:16-18).

11 WHY CHRIST BECAME MAN

It has been said that "Christianity is Christ" and that Christian theology is therefore an explanation of who Christ is and what it means to have faith in him. That is not so simple as it might seem, however. For one thing, the most important statement to be made about Jesus is mind-boggling: he is both God and man. For another, the doctrines of Christ's person pass quickly and inevitably into the area of Christ's work. So it is impossible to talk meaningfully about who Jesus is without also talking about what he did and about the importance of that for us.

Why did Jesus become man? The answer to that question, as we will see, is that Jesus became man in order to die for those who were to believe in him. Such an answer deals with the work of Christ and could therefore properly be considered later, in the section on Christ's work. But it belongs here also, for the work of Christ relates closely to who he is, and the question "What did he do?" inevitably requires an explanation of his unique nature as the God-man. We might say that the nature of Christ gives meaning to his work. And his work, centered in the atonement, is the only proper foundation for a doctrine of his person.

James Denney, a professor at the United Free Church College in Glasgow, Scotland, around the turn of the century, discusses the matter. We need an atonement. But, as Denney writes, Christ is the only person who can do this work for us. *This is the deepest and most decisive thing we can know about him, and in answering the questions which it prompts we are starting from a basis in experience. There is a sense in which Christ confronts us as the reconciler. He is doing the will of God on our behalf, and we can only look on. We see in him the judgment and the mercy of God in relation to our sins. His presence and work on earth are a divine gift, a divine visitation. He is the gift of God to men, not the offering of men to God, and God gives himself to us in and with him. We owe to him all that we call divine life. On the other hand, this divine visitation is made, and this divine life is imparted, through a life and work which are truly human. The presence and work of Jesus in the world, even the work of bearing sin, does not prompt us to define human and divine by contrast with each other: there is no suggestion of incongruity between them. Nevertheless, they are both there, and the fact that they are both there justifies us in raising the question as to Jesus' relation to God on the one hand, and to men on the other.* [1]
So the work of Christ, particularly as an explanation of the Incarnation, must occupy us here. Only after that will we be free to survey Christ's work more comprehensively.

Cur Deus Homo?

A classic statement, both the question of why Jesus Christ became man and its answer, is found in the works of Anselm of Canterbury (died 1109). Anselm's theological masterpiece, *Cur Deus Homo?* (literally "Why God Man?" or more colloquially "Why Did God Become Man?") deals with the question of the Incarnation. The answer is a carefully thought-out statement of the atonement. Anselm answered that God became man in Christ because only one who was both God and man could achieve our salvation. In approaching the subject from Anselm's perspective, we do not want to say that there are no other reasons for the Incarnation. We have already noted that it reveals the value set by God upon human life. Life is declared to be valuable by the creation alone, but sin has cheapened life. The Incarnation, coming in the midst of a history of human sin, indicates that God has not abandoned us but loves us and values us even in our fallen state. The Incarnation does two further things. It shows us that God is able to understand us and sympathize with us, which is an inducement to come to him in prayer (as suggested in the last chapter). Also, the Incarnation gives an example of how a person ought to live in this world. Peter refers even to the crucifixion in such terms: "Christ also suffered for you, leaving you an example, that you should follow in his steps" (1 Pet. 2:21).

But the atonement is the real reason for the Incarnation. The author of Hebrews affirms this clearly. "It is impossible that the blood of bulls and goats should take away sins. Consequently, when Christ came into the world, he said, 'Sacrifices and offerings thou hast not desired, but a body hast thou prepared for me; in burnt offerings and sin offerings thou hast taken no pleasure. Then I said, "Lo, I have come to do thy will, O God," as it is written of me in the roll of the book' " (Heb. 10:4-7). The writer then adds that when Jesus says he is coming to do God's will, that will must be understood as the providing of a better sacrifice. "And by that will we have been sanctified through the offering of the body of Jesus Christ once for all" (10:10).

We find the same emphasis elsewhere. In its derivation the name *Jesus* ("Jehovah saves") looks forward to the atonement: "You shall call his name Jesus, for he will save his people from their sins" (Mt. 1:21). Jesus himself spoke of his coming suffering (Mk. 8:31; 9:31), linking the success of his mission to the crucifixion: "And I, when I am lifted up from the earth, will draw all men to myself" (Jn. 12:32). At several places in John's Gospel the crucifixion is spoken of as that vital "hour" for which Christ came (Jn. 2:4; 7:30; 8:20; 12:23, 27; 13:1; 17:1).

Moreover, the death of Jesus is the theme of the Old Testament also, first in regard to the full meaning of the sacrifices (the meaning at the heart of the law) and then in regard to the prophecies, which focused increasingly on the promise of a coming redeemer. Isaiah 53 and other Old Testament texts speak of the suffering of the deliverer to come. In Galatians the apostle Paul teaches that even Abraham, who lived before both the law and prophets, was saved by faith in Jesus (Gal. 3:8, 16). Jesus taught the downcast Emmaus disciples that the Old Testament foretold his death and resurrection: "He said to them, 'O foolish men, and slow of heart to believe all that the prophets have spoken! Was it not necessary that the Christ should suffer these things and enter into his glory?' And beginning with Moses and all the prophets, he interpreted to them in all the scriptures the things concerning himself" (Lk. 24:25-27). In the light of these texts and many others, it is necessary to say that the atonement of Christ is *the* reason for the Incarnation. It is the explanation of his twofold nature and the focal point of world and biblical history.

Man Owed It; Only God Could Pay It

Why must the doctrine of the atonement be central to the Scriptures? Why must there even be a sacrifice? Or, granting that an atonement is needed, why must Jesus, the God-man, be the one to provide it? One answer, which Calvin gives in the *Institutes of the Christian Religion,* is that this is how God has chosen to do it and that it is therefore impertinent of us to ask if there could not be some other way. But that is not a full answer, as both Calvin and Anselm recognized. It is possible to ask without impertinence, in an effort to seek understanding, why salvation had to be achieved in this way.[2]

Anselm (and Calvin after him) gave two answers. The first is that salvation had to be achieved by God, for no one else could achieve it. Certainly men and women could not achieve it, for we are the ones who have gotten ourselves into trouble in the first place. We have done so by our rebellion against God's just law and decrees. Moreover, we have suffered from the effects of sin to such a degree that our will is bound, and therefore we cannot even choose to please God, let alone actually please him. If we are to be saved, only God, who has both the will and power to save, must save us. Anselm's second answer is that, in apparent contradiction, salvation must also be achieved by man. Man is the one who has wronged God and must therefore make the wrong right. Granted this state of affairs, salvation can be achieved only by one who is both God and man, namely, by Christ.

> *It would not have been right for the restoration of human nature to be left undone, and . . . it could not have been done unless man paid what was owing to God for sin. But the debt was so great that, while man alone owed it, only God could pay it, so that the same person must be both man and God. Thus it was necessary for God to take manhood into the unity of his person, so that he who in his own nature ought to pay and could not should be in a person who could. . . . The life of this man was so sublime, so precious, that it can suffice to pay what is owing for the sins of the whole world, and infinitely more.*[3]

Three points must be remembered if Anselm's explanation of the Incarnation is not to be misunderstood. First, it is God who initiates and carries out the action. If that is forgotten, it is easy to think of God as being somehow remote from the atonement and therefore merely requiring it as some abstract price paid to satisfy his justice. In that view God appears disinterested, legalistic and cruel. Actually, God's nature is characterized by love, and it is out of love that he planned and carried out the atonement. In Christ God himself was satisfying his own justice. So it is easy to see why the Incarnation and the atonement must be considered together if each is not to be distorted.

Second, in Anselm's explanation there is no suggestion whatever of human beings somehow placating the wrath of an angry God. Propitiation does refer to the placating of wrath, as will be seen in the study of that concept in chapter thirteen. But it is not man who placates God. Rather it is God placating his own wrath so that his love might go out to embrace and fully save the sinner.

Third, it is not a matter of substitution in the bald sense in which an innocent victim takes the place of another person who should be punished. Rather, it is substitution in a deeper sense. The one who takes the place of man in order to satisfy God's justice is actually one who had himself become man and is therefore what we might term our representative.

A proper recognition of the connection between the Incarnation and the atonement makes the Incarnation understandable. At the same time it eliminates the most common misunderstandings of, and objections to, Christ's sacrifice of himself as the means of our salvation. One writer summarizes the matter like this:

God is not only perfectly holy, but the source and pattern of holiness: He is the origin and the upholder of the moral order of the universe. He must be just. The Judge of all the earth must do right. Therefore it was impossible by the necessities of his own being that he should deal lightly with sin, and compromise the claims of holiness. If sin could be forgiven at all, it must be on some basis which would vindicate the holy law of God, which is not a mere code, but the moral order of the whole creation. But such vindication must be supremely costly. Costly to whom? Not to the forgiven sinner, for there could be no price asked from him for his forgiveness; both because the cost is far beyond his reach, and because God loves to give and not to sell. Therefore God himself undertook to pay a cost, to offer a sacrifice, so tremendous that the gravity of his condem-

nation of sin should be absolutely beyond question even as he for-
gave it, while at the same time the Love which impelled him to pay
the price would be the wonder of angels, and would call forth the
worshipping gratitude of the redeemed sinner.

On Calvary this price was paid, paid by God: *the Son giving*
himself, bearing our sin and its curse; the Father giving the Son,
his only Son whom he loved. But it was paid by God become man,
who not only took the place of guilty man, but also was his repre-
sentative. . . .

The divine Son, one of the three persons of the one God, he
through whom, from the beginning of the creation, the Father has
revealed himself to man (John 1:18), took man's nature upon him,
and so became our representative. He offered himself as a sacrifice
in our stead, bearing our sin in his own body on the tree. He suf-
fered, not only awful physical anguish, but also the unthinkable
spiritual horror of becoming identified with the sin to which he was
infinitely opposed. He thereby came under the curse of sin, so that
for a time even his perfect fellowship with his Father was broken.
Thus God proclaimed his infinite abhorrence of sin by being willing
himself to suffer all that, in place of the guilty ones, in order that
he might justly forgive. Thus the love of God found its perfect
fulfillment, because he did not hold back from even that uttermost
sacrifice, in order that we might be saved from eternal death
through what he endured. Thus it was possible for him to be just,
and to justify the believer, because as Lawgiver and as Substitute
for the rebel race of man, he himself had suffered the penalty of
the broken law.[4]

Steps to Calvary

Several conclusions flow from this explanation of the Incarnation. First, according to the Scriptures Calvary and not
Bethlehem is the center of Christianity. An idea popular in
some theological circles has been that the Incarnation is the
most important thing, that is, God identifying himself with
man, and that the atonement was something like an after-

thought. But according to the biblical teaching, the reason for the God-man is that it required a God-man to die for our salvation. Therefore, "The crucial significance of the cradle at Bethlehem lies in its place in the sequence of steps down that led the Son of God to the cross of Calvary, and we do not understand it till we see it in this context."[5] To focus on the Incarnation apart from the cross leads to false sentimentality and neglect of the horror and magnitude of human sin.

Second, if the death of Christ on the cross is the true meaning of the Incarnation, then there is no gospel without the cross. Christmas by itself is no gospel. The life of Christ is no gospel. Even the resurrection, important as it is in the total scheme of things, is no gospel by itself. For the good news is not just that God became man, nor that God has spoken to reveal a proper way of life to us, or even that death, the great enemy, is conquered. Rather, the good news is that sin has been dealt with (of which the resurrection is a proof); that Jesus has suffered its penalty for us as our representative, so that we might never have to suffer it; and that therefore all who believe in him can look forward to heaven. Moreover, the other biblical themes must be seen in that context, as we have already seen of the Incarnation. Emulation of Christ's life and teaching is possible only to those who enter into a new relationship with God through faith in Jesus as their substitute. The resurrection is not merely a victory over death (though it is that) but a proof that the atonement was a satisfactory atonement in the sight of the Father (Rom. 4:25); and that death, the result of sin, is abolished on that basis.

Any gospel that talks merely of the Christ-event, meaning the Incarnation without the atonement, is a false gospel. Any gospel that talks about the love of God without pointing out that his love led him to pay the ultimate price for sin in the person of his Son on the cross is a false gospel. The only true gospel is the gospel of the "one mediator" (1 Tim. 2:5-6), who gave himself for us.

Finally, just as there can be no gospel without the atonement as the reason for the Incarnation, so also there can be no Christian life without it. Without the atonement the Incarnation theme easily becomes a kind of deification of the human and leads to arrogance and self-advancement. With the atonement the true message of the life of Christ, and therefore also of the life of the Christian man or woman, is humility and self-sacrifice for the obvious needs of others. The Christian life is not indifference to those who are hungry or sick or suffering from some other lack. It is not contentment with our own abundance, neither the abundance of middle-class living with homes and cars and clothes and vacations, nor the abundance of education nor even the spiritual abundance of good churches, Bibles, Bible teaching or Christian friends and acquaintances. Rather, it is the awareness that others lack these things and that we must therefore sacrifice many of our own interests in order to identify with them and thus bring them increasingly into the abundance we enjoy.

Paul wrote of the Incarnation: "For you know the grace of our Lord Jesus Christ, that though he was rich, yet for your sake he became poor, so that by his poverty you might become rich" (2 Cor. 8:9). That is also a statement of the atonement and of the Christian life. In fact, it occurs in a chapter in which Paul is speaking about the duty of the Christians at Corinth to give money for the relief of those less fortunate who lived in Judea. We will live for Christ fully only when we are willing to be impoverished, if necessary, in order that others might be helped.

PART IV
THE WORK OF CHRIST

Jesus of Nazareth, who was a prophet mighty in deed and word. (Lk. 24:19)

Therefore he had to be made like his brethren in every respect, so that he might become a merciful and faithful high priest in the service of God, to make expiation for the sins of the people. (Heb. 2:17)

King of kings and Lord of lords. (Rev. 19:16)

They are justified by his grace as a gift, through the redemption which is in Christ Jesus, whom God put forward as an expiation by his blood, to be received by faith. (Rom. 3:24-25)

For God so loved the world that he gave his only Son, that whoever believes in him should not perish but have eternal life. (Jn. 3:16)

For I delivered to you as of first importance what I also received, that Christ died for our sins in accordance with the scriptures, that he was buried, that he was raised on the third day in accordance with the scriptures, and that he appeared to Cephas, then to the twelve. Then he appeared to more than five hundred brethren at one time.... Then he appeared to James, then to all the apostles. Last of all, as to one untimely born, he appeared also to me. (1 Cor. 15:3-8)

12

PROPHET, PRIEST AND KING

It has been common in Protestant circles since the Reformation to speak of the work of Christ under three general heads: prophet, priest and king. These refer to his roles as teacher, Savior and ruler over the universe and the church. It has been objected by some that these roles are not always that distinct, either in Christ's own ministry or in the Old Testament offices upon which they are built. Priests as well as prophets are found to be teachers. Several kings were recipients of God's inspired revelation, as were the prophets. Nevertheless, the usual threefold division of Christ's work has good scriptural support.

Christ is acknowledged to be a prophet in Luke 24:19. In that passage Jesus is interrogating the Emmaus disciples, asking what had happened during the last tumultuous days in Jerusalem. They reply that those events concern "Jesus of Nazareth, who was a prophet mighty in deed and word before God and all the people."

Jesus is declared to be a priest throughout the book of

Hebrews as, for example in Hebrews 2:17. "Therefore he had to be made like his brethren in every respect, so that he might become a merciful and faithful high priest in the service of God, to make expiation for the sins of the people."

Similarly, Revelation 19:16 declares, "On his robe and on his thigh he has a name inscribed, King of kings and Lord of lords."

The notion of the threefold office of Christ also applies well to human spiritual need. One such need is for knowledge; we do not know God naturally, nor do we understand spiritual things apart from special divine illumination of our minds. Jesus meets our need by revealing God to us. He is our prophet-teacher. He does this through his own person, in whom the Father is fully revealed; through the gift to us of the written Word of God; and by the particular illumination of our minds by the Holy Spirit.

We also have need of salvation. We are not merely ignorant of God and of spiritual things; we are also sinful. We have rebelled against God and like sheep have all gone our own way. Jesus meets this need as our priest. He functions as priest on two levels: first, he offers himself up as a sacrifice, thereby providing the perfect atonement for our sin; second, he intercedes for us at the right hand of his Father in heaven, thereby guaranteeing our right to be heard.

Finally, we need spiritual discipline, guidance and rule. We are not autonomous, even after our conversion. We do not have the right to rule ourselves, nor can we rule ourselves successfully. Christ meets our need by his proper and loving rule over us within the church. He is our master, our king. He is also the proper ruler of this world, a rule he will assume eventually. Hence the future triumph and rule of Christ over all the world is also an aspect of this subject. Summing the matter up, Charles Hodge has said:

We are enlightened in the knowledge of the truth; we are reconciled unto God by the sacrificial death of his Son; and we are de-

livered from the power of Satan and introduced into the kingdom of God; all of which supposes that our Redeemer is to us at once prophet, priest, and king. This is not, therefore, simply a convenient classification of the contents of his mission and work, but it enters into its very nature, and must be retained in our theology if we would take the truth as it is revealed in the Word of God.[1]
Therefore, although our discussion of the work of Christ will necessarily go beyond what these three categories suggest, it will nevertheless be of value to keep them in mind as we develop it.

The Logos of God

When we talk about Christ's prophetic office we go back to a particularly rich lode of thought in the Old Testament. Abraham, the father of the Jewish people, was called a prophet (Gen. 20:7). Moses was a prophet, even the greatest of all prophets (Deut. 34:10). Saul prophesied (1 Sam. 10:11; 19:20). David and Solomon were prophets in the sense that they received parts of God's inspired revelation and have thus contributed to our Old Testament. Beginning with Elijah and Elisha the great prophetic movement was launched, bringing into view such names as Isaiah, Jeremiah, Ezekiel, Daniel and the so-called minor prophets. On one occasion Moses is reported as saying, "Would that all the LORD's people were prophets!" (Num. 11:29).

In the midst of the focus on the role of the prophet there is, however, an increasing awareness that no human prophet is adequate for human need. Therefore there is a sharpening expectation of one "great prophet" who should come.

The first clear statement of that expectation is in Deuteronomy 18 which contains a prophecy of a future prophetic figure like Moses, one to whom the people should hearken. Moses himself makes the announcement: "The LORD your God will raise up for you a prophet like me from among you, from your brethren—him you shall heed" (Deut. 18:15).

Then the announcement is preserved in God's own words: "I will raise up for them a prophet like you from among their brethren; and I will put my words in his mouth, and he shall speak to them all that I command him" (Deut. 18:18). It is possible on a superficial reading to take this as referring to some subsequent human figure, such as Isaiah or one of the other great prophets. It might even be applied to that special prophet who was to be the forerunner of the Messiah (Mal. 4:5; Jn. 1:25). In the New Testament itself the Deuteronomy reference is applied explicitly to Jesus, as in one of Peter's sermons (Acts 3:22) and Stephen's address before the Sanhedrin (Acts 7:37).

Other passages develop the same theme. On several occasions the people who witnessed a striking work of Christ responded by identifying him as a prophet or *the* prophet to be expected in the last times (Mt. 21:46; Lk. 7:16; Jn. 6:14). The Emmaus disciples identified him as such (Lk. 24:19). On one occasion Jesus said in reference to himself, "A prophet is not without honor, except in his own country, and among his own kin, and in his own house" (Mk. 6:4). From a theological standpoint the major passage is probably the introduction to the book of Hebrews. "In many and various ways God spoke of old to our fathers by the prophets; but in these last days he has spoken to us by a Son" (Heb. 1:1-2).

A prophet is one who speaks for another. In these verses Jesus is set forth as one who, like the Old Testament prophets, speaks for God. He is thus one who speaks authoritatively.

The matter of *authority* was particularly evident to Christ's hearers. At the end of the Sermon on the Mount we are told that when Jesus had finished speaking, the people were "astonished at his teaching, for he taught them as one who had authority, and not as their scribes" (Mt. 7:28-29). We might think that they should have been impressed with the content of his words, or with the need for repentance, or some such thing. But we are told that the people contrasted Christ with the scribes, who were the major teachers of the time, and concluded that he was teaching with an authority they did not possess.

A second major feature of Christ's teaching is what we might call its *egocentric* character. It is about himself. As early as his words about persecution in the Sermon on the Mount, Jesus assumes that his hearers would experience suffering not merely for the sake of truth or for some other good cause but "on my account" (Mt. 5:11). Later in the sermon he says, "Think not that I have come to abolish the law and the prophets; I have come not to abolish them but to fulfil them" (Mt. 5:17). In other words, he identified himself as the Messiah about whom the Old Testament was written. In the final section he warns against anything that might turn attention from himself and thus lead the person involved into judgment. He concludes, "Every one then who hears these words of mine and does them will be like a wise man who built his house upon the rock; and the rain fell, and the floods came, and the winds blew and beat upon that house, but it did not fall, because it had been founded on the rock" (Mt. 7:24-25).

These statements, and others like them throughout the Gospels, immediately distinguish Jesus from all other religious teachers. As John R.W. Stott observes: "They are self-effacing; he is self-advancing. They point away from themselves and say, 'That is the truth as far as I perceive it; follow that.' Jesus says, 'I am the truth; follow me.' "[2]

The fourth evangelist, John, was apparently very conscious of this aspect of Christ's teaching as he began to write his Gospel. In the opening pages he uses a word in reference to Christ which suggested both to Jews and Greeks that Christ himself was the focal point of God's revelation to men. The word is *logos,* which means "word," though in a fuller sense than is true of that term in English. It occurs in verse 1, where John says, "In the beginning was the Word, and the Word was with God, and the Word was God," and in verse 14, "And the

Word became flesh and dwelt among us, full of grace and truth."

What would that term have meant to a contemporary Jewish reader of John's Gospel? The first verses of his book, including the term *logos,* would have made a Jew think back to the first words of the Old Testament where we are told that in the beginning God spoke and that as a result all things came into being. In other words, Jesus would immediately be associated with the creative power of God and with the self-disclosure of God in creation. We can get a feeling for how this might operate by imagining ourselves to be reading a book which began with a reference to "the course of human events" and contained in the first few paragraphs the words "self-evident" and "inalienable rights." Clearly the author would be trying to remind us of the Declaration of Independence and of the founding principles of the American republic.

But that is not all these words would do for a Jewish reader. To a Jewish mind the idea of a "word" would mean more than it does to us today. The reason is that to the Jewish way of thinking a word was something concrete, something much closer to what we would call an event or a deed. We say, "Words are cheap." Children chant, "Sticks and stones may break my bones, but words will never hurt me!" But words do hurt, and the Jews were undoubtedly closer to the truth when they regarded a word spoken as a deed done. To their way of thinking, words were not to be used lightly. Moreover, there are theological implications. What happens when God speaks? The thing is accomplished instantly. "God said, 'Let there be light'; and there was light" (Gen. 1:3). God said, "So shall my word be that goes forth from my mouth; it shall not return to me empty, but it shall accomplish that which I purpose, and prosper in the thing for which I sent it" (Is. 55:11). Because of this the Jews would be more prepared than we are for the thought that the "Word" of God could somehow be seen and touched, and it would not be entirely strange for them to learn, as the author of Hebrews said in writing to largely Jewish readers, "In these last days [God] has spoken to us by a Son" (Heb. 1:2).

What would the word *logos* have meant to a Greek or other gentile reader? For the Greeks the answer is found, not in religion, but in philosophy. Almost twenty-six hundred years ago, in the sixth century B.C., a philosopher named Heraclitus lived in Ephesus. He was the man who said that it is impossible to step into the same river twice. He meant that all of life is in a state of change. Thus, although you step into the river once, step out, and then step in a second time, by the time you have taken the second step the river has flowed on and is a different river. To Heraclitus and to the philosophers who followed him, all of life seemed like that. But they asked, if that is so, how is it that everything that exists is not in a state of perpetual chaos? Heraclitus answered that life is not chaos because the change that we see is not random change. It is ordered change. That means that there must be a divine "reason" or "word" that controls it. That is the *logos,* the word that John uses in the opening verse of his Gospel.

However, the *logos* also meant more than that to Heraclitus. Once he had discovered that the controlling principle of matter was God's *logos,* then it was only a small step for him to apply that concept also to all the events of history and to the mental order that rules in the minds of human beings. For Heraclitus the *logos* became nothing less than the mind of God controlling everything.

By the time John came to write his Gospel, the age of Heraclitus lay nearly seven hundred years in the past. But Heraclitus's ideas had been so formative for Greek thought that they had survived not only in his philosophy but also in the philosophy of Plato and Socrates, the Stoics, and others who had built upon it. Further, they were discussed by many ordinary persons. The Greek knew all about the *logos.* For him the *logos* was the creative and controlling mind of God; it kept the universe going. It was therefore with a stroke of divine genius that John seized upon this word, one that was as meaningful to Greeks as to the Jewish people. "Listen, you Greeks, the very thing that has most occupied your philosophical thought and about which you have all been writing for centuries—the Logos of God, this word, this controlling power of the universe and man's mind—this has now come to earth as a man, and we have beheld him, full of grace and truth."

Plato, we are told, once turned to that little group of philosophers and students that had gathered around him during the Golden Age in Athens and said, "It may be that some day there will come forth from God a Word, a Logos, who will reveal all mysteries and make everything plain." Now John is saying, "Yes, Plato, the Logos has come; now God is revealed to us perfectly."[3]

This is the prophetic ministry of Jesus Christ. It is authoritative, and it is wrapped up in his own person in such a way that when we look to Jesus we see, not merely a man, but the God-man who thereby reveals God to us. In our day Jesus performs this ministry through his Holy Spirit who communicates the person of Christ to our minds and hearts through the Scriptures and thus provides for our salvation and sanctification.

The Mediator of God: Priest

The second of the three major divisions of Christ's work is his priesthood, a theme carefully prepared for in the Old Testament and developed in considerable detail in the book of Hebrews. A priest is a man appointed to act for others in things pertaining to God. That is, he is a mediator. In Christ this priestly or mediatorial function is fulfilled in two ways: first, by offering up himself as a sacrifice for sin (which the Old Testament priests could not do) and, second, by interceding for his people in heaven. The New Testament represents this last activity as Christ urging the sufficiency of his sacrifice as grounds upon which his prayers and ours should be answered.

The fact that Jesus is himself the sacrifice for sins should make it clear that his priesthood is different from and superior to the Old Testament priestly functions. But not only in this regard is Christ superior. To begin with, under the Old Testament system the priests of Israel were required to offer a sacrifice not only for those whom they represented but also for themselves, since they were sinful. For example, before the high priest could go into the Holy of Holies on the Day of Atonement, which he did once a year, he first had to offer a bullock as a burnt offering for his own sin and that of his household (Lev. 16:6). Only after that was he able to proceed with the ceremonies of the scapegoat and the offering whose blood was to be sprinkled upon the mercy seat within the Holy of Holies. Again, the sacrifices that the priests of Israel offered were inadequate. They taught the way of salvation through the death of an innocent victim. But the blood of sheep and goats could not take away sins, as both the Old Testament and the New Testament recognize (Mic. 6:6-7; Heb. 10:4-7). Finally, the sacrifices of the earthly priests were incomplete, which is attested to by the fact that they were offered again and again. In Jerusalem, for example, the fire on the great altar of sacrifice never went out; and on a great sabbath, such as the Passover, literally hundreds of thousands of lambs would be offered.

In contrast to that earthly priesthood, _the sacrifice of Jesus was by one who is himself perfect_ and who therefore had no need that atonement be made for him. As the author of Hebrews says, "It was fitting that we should have such a high priest, holy, blameless, unstained, separated from sinners, exalted above the heavens. He has no need, like those high priests, to offer sacrifices daily, first for his own sins and then for those of the people" (Heb. 7:26-27).

Second, being himself perfect and at the same time the sacrifice, it follows that *the sacrifice made by Jesus was itself perfect.* Hence, it could actually pay the price for sin and remove it, as the sacrifices in Israel could not. They were a shadow of things to come, but they were not the reality. Christ's death was the actual atonement on the basis of which alone God declares the sinner righteous. The author of Hebrews makes this point. "But when Christ appeared as a high priest of the good things that have come . . . he entered once for all into the Holy Place, taking not the blood of goats and calves but his own blood, thus securing an eternal redemption. For if the sprinkling of defiled persons with the blood of goats and bulls and with the ashes of a heifer sanctifies for the purification of the flesh, how much more shall the blood of Christ, who through the eternal Spirit offered himself without blemish to God, purify your conscience from dead works to serve the living God" (Heb. 9:11-14).

Finally, unlike the sacrifices of the Old Testament priests, which had to be repeated daily, *the sacrifice of Jesus was complete and eternal*—as evidence for which he is now seated at the right hand of God. In the Jewish temple there were no chairs, signifying that the work of the priests was never done. "But when Christ had offered for all time a single sacrifice for sins, he sat down at the right hand of God, then to wait until his enemies should be made a stool for his feet. For by a single offering he has perfected for all time those who are sanctified" (Heb. 10:12-14).

Any teaching about priests and sacrifices today is hard for most people to understand, for we do not have sacrifice in most of the civilized world and do not understand its terminology. It was not so easy to understand in antiquity either. The author of Hebrews, in fact, acknowledges that in a parenthetical remark: "About this we have much to say which is hard to explain, since you have become dull of hearing" (Heb. 5:11).

On the other hand, the elaborate instructions for the performances of sacrifices were given to teach both the serious nature of sin and the way God would provide for sin to be dealt with. The sacrifices taught two lessons. First, sin means death. It is a lesson of God's judgment. It means that sin is serious. "The soul that sins shall die" (Ezek. 18:4). Second, there is the message of grace. The significance of the sacrifice is that by the grace of God an innocent substitute could be offered in the sinner's place. The goat or lamb was not that substitute, but could only point forward to it. Jesus was and is, for all who will have him as Savior. He is the only, perfect, all-sufficient sacrifice for sin on the basis of which God counts the sinner justified. This aspect of Christ's work is to be considered more fully in the chapters on propitiation and redemption.

A second way in which Jesus fulfills his priestly or mediatorial function is by interceding for us now. This is not a supplemental work adding to his sacrifice of himself on the cross but rather a consequential work based upon it. We have several examples of Christ's intercession for others in the New Testament.

One interesting example is his intercession for Peter, told after the fact. The story is that Satan came to God on one occasion and gave his opinion of Peter, saying in effect, "I don't know what your Son ever expects to accomplish with that bag of wind named Peter. If you would just give me permission to blow on him, he'd fly away like chaff at threshing time." At that point God gave Satan permission to blow, just as he had given Satan permission to blow on Job (Job 1:12; 2:6). But Jesus prayed for Peter, asking that the experience might prove strengthening rather than devastating. He asked that the chaff might be blown away so that more of the true grain, which he had put there, might be visible. His own words to Peter were "Simon, Simon, behold, Satan demanded to have you, that he might sift you like wheat, but I have prayed for you that your faith may not fail; and when you have turned again, strengthen your brethren" (Lk. 22:31-32).

We know from the outworking of the story that Christ's intercession for Peter prevailed. Later that evening, although Peter denied the Lord on three separate occasions, the last time with oaths and cursing, his faith did not fail. Rather, when what he had done became clear to him through the crowing of the cock, remorse overcame him and he went out and wept bitterly. It was to a greatly humbled Peter that the Lord later came with a recommissioning to service (Jn. 21: 15-19).

Another New Testament example of Christ's intercession is his prayer for his church (Jn. 17). Jesus does not pray that the disciples might be made rich or be brought to positions of respect and power in the Roman Empire or even be spared persecution and suffering for the sake of their witness. Rather, his prayer is that they might be made the kind of men and women he would have them be; that is, men and women in whom the marks of the church are evident: joy, holiness, truth, mission, unity and love. His concerns for them (and us) are spiritual.

A wonderful word is used for this mediatorial function of the Lord Jesus Christ, doubly wonderful because it is also used of the earthly ministry of the Holy Spirit on our behalf. In the Greek language the word is *paraklētos.* In English it is translated "Comforter" (though that is not the best translation), "Counselor" or "Advocate." It is used of the Holy Spirit in Christ's final discourses, in which he speaks of "another Counselor" (Jn. 14:16; cf. 14:26; 15:26; 16:7). It is used of Jesus himself (1 Jn. 2:1). The real sense of the word comes from its legal or forensic overtones. Literally, *paraklētos* comes from two separate Greek words: *para,* meaning "alongside of" (we have it in the words *parable, paradox, parallel,* and others), and *klētos,* meaning "called" (it is also used in the Greek word for church, *ekklēsia,* meaning "the called out ones"). A paraclete is therefore one called alongside another to help him, in

other words, a lawyer. Interestingly enough, that is the meaning of the word _advocate. Advocate_ is composed of the two
words, _ad,_ meaning "to" or "towards," and _vocare,_ "to call." So
an advocate is one called to help another.

The picture, then, is of something we might call a heavenly
law firm with us as clients. It has a heavenly branch presided
over by the Lord Jesus Christ and an earthly branch directed
by the Holy Spirit. Each of them pleads for us. It is the Spirit's
role to move us to pray and to intensify that prayer to a point
of which we ourselves are not capable. Paul writes, "Likewise
the Spirit helps us in our weakness; for we do not know how
to pray as we ought, but the Spirit himself intercedes for us
with sighs too deep for words" (Rom. 8:26). Similarly, it is the
ministry of the Lord in heaven to interpret our prayers aright
and plead the efficacy of his sacrifice as the basis of our coming to God.

The consequence of this is that we can have great boldness
in prayer. How could we ever have boldness if the answering
of our prayers depended either upon the strength with which
we pray or upon the correctness of the petitions themselves?
Our prayers are weak, as Paul confesses, and we often pray
wrongly. But we are bold, nevertheless, for we have the Holy
Spirit to strengthen the requests, and the Lord Jesus Christ
to interpret them rightly.

The Reign of God: King
The third aspect of Christ's work is kingship. Unlike the two
other offices which have a limited, explicit, textual basis, there
is voluminous biblical material on Christ's kingship.

First, there is the strong theme of the sovereignty of God
over his creation. Since Jesus is himself God, that clearly has
bearing on his own rule or sovereignty. There are the particular messianic prophecies about the Messiah's kingly reign, as
God promised King David. "Your house and your kingdom
shall be made sure for ever before me; your throne shall be

established for ever" (2 Sam. 7:16). Later, when the house of David was in evident decline, the prophet Isaiah intensified the promises and pointed to the Messiah yet to come. "The government will be upon his shoulder, and his name will be called 'Wonderful Counselor, Mighty God, Everlasting Father, Prince of Peace.' Of the increase of his government and of peace there will be no end, upon the throne of David, and over his kingdom, to establish it, and to uphold it with justice and with righteousness from this time forth and for evermore. The zeal of the LORD of hosts will do this" (Is. 9:6-7). Many psalms are given over to the theme (for example, Ps. 45; 72; 110). Micah 5:2 speaks of the birthplace of this future king: "But you, O Bethlehem Ephrathah, who are little to be among the clans of Judah, from you shall come forth for me one who is to be ruler in Israel, whose origin is from of old, from ancient days." Daniel contains a vision of one to whom "was given dominion and glory and kingdom, that all peoples, nations, and languages should serve him; his dominion is an everlasting dominion, which shall not pass away, and his kingdom one that shall not be destroyed" (Dan. 7:13-14).

When Jesus was born his birth was announced in these categories, and when he began his earthly ministry he himself played on these themes. The angel who announced his birth to Mary said, "He will be great, and will be called the Son of the Most High; and the Lord God will give to him the throne of his father David, and he will reign over the house of Jacob for ever; and of his kingdom there will be no end" (Lk. 1:32-33). Later John the Baptist spoke of the imminence of God's kingdom in the coming of Christ. Still later Jesus himself began his ministry with the startling proclamation, "Repent, for the kingdom of heaven is at hand" (Mt. 4:17).

At the end of the New Testament we find the culmination of this theme: the Lord seated upon a throne, his enemies being made subject to him and a new name given. "On his robe and on his thigh he has a name inscribed, King of kings and Lord of lords" (Rev. 19:16).

Here a problem develops. If this theme is as dominant as it seems and if Jesus really is the King of kings and Lord of lords, how is it that the world is so little changed and that his kingdom is so little acknowledged? Is it future? That would be one way to handle the problem, but how do we then deal with Christ's own statement that the kingdom of God is "in the midst of you" (Lk. 17:21)? Is it spiritual? If so, how are we to think of the explicit prophecies of the continuation of the throne of David or even the promises of utopian justice and peace to attend Messiah's reign? We note, for instance, that the lack of justice and peace in the world is one reason given by today's Jewish community for their refusal to believe that Jesus of Nazareth is their true Messiah. Can we eliminate these elements from our understanding of Christ's rule? Or are we to limit the kingship of Jesus to the church alone? The answers to each of these questions are complex, but it is only as we ask them and begin to search for answers in the Bible that we come by degrees actually to understand the concept of Christ's kingship.

I was once asked a question about whether the kingdom of God is past, present or future. The questioner had in mind the debate on that subject going on in scholarly theological circles for some years, involving such names as T. W. Manson and C. H. Dodd of England, Rudolph Bultmann and Martin Dibelius of Germany, and Albert Schweitzer. I replied with a summary of that debate and then with the statement that the biblical view could not be expressed adequately even in those three terms. In one sense the kingdom is certainly past, for God has always ruled over people and history. But at the same time it is also present and future. Thus God rules today and will continue to rule. The more one looks at the statements in the Bible about the kingdom, the more one feels that it transcends any of these temporal concepts.

Perhaps the most important thing to be said about the kingdom of God is that it is *God's* kingdom. That means it is far above the kingdoms of men and is infinitely superior to them.

We look into the pages of history and we see the kingdoms of this world rising and falling across the centuries. Historians tell us that the world has known twenty-one great civilizations, all of which have endured only for a time and then passed away unceremoniously. Once Egypt was a mighty world power, but today it is weak. It is unable to contend even with the tiny state of Israel. Babylon was mighty. Today it is gone, its territory divided. Syria, once strong, has become an archaeological curiosity. Greece and Rome have fallen. Moreover, we know that even the United States of America and the Soviet Union, although now at the pinnacle of world power, will not be able to escape that inexorable law of God for history: "Righteousness exalts a nation, but sin is a reproach to any people" (Prov. 14:34). Pride can bring each of them down.

The normal course of the kingdoms of this world is described in a striking way in the book of Daniel. Belshazzar, king of Babylon, had given a party in the course of which he had defiled the vessels taken from the temple of God at Jerusalem. In the midst of that party, handwriting had appeared on the wall of the palace, and Belshazzar was frightened. The writing said, "MENE, MENE, TEKEL, and PARSIN. This is the interpretation of the matter: MENE, God has numbered the days of your kingdom and brought it to an end; TEKEL, you have been weighed in the balances, and found wanting; PERES, your kingdom is divided and given to the Medes and Persians" (Dan. 5:25-28). Daniel said to the king,

"The Most High God gave Nebuchadnezzar your father kingship and greatness and glory and majesty. . . . But when his heart was lifted up and his spirit was hardened so that he dealt proudly, he was deposed from his kingly throne, and his glory was taken from him; he was driven from among men, and his mind was made like that of a beast, and his dwelling was with the wild asses; he was fed grass like an ox, and his body was wet with the dew of heaven,

*until he knew that the Most High God rules the kingdom of men,
and sets over it whom he will. And you his son, Belshazzar, have not
humbled your heart, though you knew all this." (Dan. 5:18, 20-22)*
That night Belshazzar was killed and Darius reigned in his
stead.

That is the course of human kingdoms. God allows an individual or group to rise above their peers in power, their triumph brings pride and God removes them. Human powers
rise and fall, but over all this seething about in human history
God reigns. God is sovereign over human history, even over
realms that are in rebellion against him. This aspect of "the
kingdom of God" brings comfort to those who would otherwise be in turmoil about upsetting world events. Jesus said,
"Do not be anxious about your life" (Mt. 6:25-34), adding that
although there would always be "wars and rumors of wars,"
his followers were not to be troubled (Mt. 24:6).

A second important fact about Christ's rule is that it has a
present dimension. Jesus first exercises his rule of an individual soul by drawing it to faith in himself and directing it
thereafter and, second, by governing and directing his church
so that the principles of the kingdom might be seen in the
church and then move out from it to have bearing on the unbelieving world. When we pray "Thy kingdom come," as we
do in the Lord's Prayer, it is this present rule (and not merely
a future coming) that we have in mind. Paul defines the kingdom of God as a present-tense reality: "righteousness and
peace and joy in the Holy Spirit" (Rom. 14:17).

Unfortunately, some have gone on from an awareness of
Christ's expanding rule over his church and the world to
make the erroneous assumption that because the kingdom of
God comes wherever individuals believe in Christ and respond to the gospel, the kingdom will therefore inevitably go
on expanding until all or nearly all the world believes. That
view was popular in the nineteenth century. Today the reality
of two world wars, a cold war, and the acknowledged decline

of the influence of Christianity in the Western world have taken the enthusiasm for that sort of reasoning out of most Christians.

It is surprising that such a line of thought was followed at all. The Lord warned against it in the parables of the kingdom (Mt. 13), teaching that large portions of the world would never be converted, that the devil's children would be present until the end even in the church, that his rule would come in totality only at the close of time, and that even then it would be established only by his power and in spite of continuing and bitter animosity. There are seven parables in that chapter, beginning with the sower who went forth to sow and ending with the story of the dragnet. They are designed to preview the last nineteen centuries of church history.

The first parable is the parable of the sower. Jesus said that a man went out to sow seed. Some of it fell on a hard surface where it was devoured by birds; some of it fell on shallow ground and sprang up quickly only to be scorched by the sun; some fell among thorns and was choked by them; some fell on good ground where it produced in some cases a hundred handfuls of grain for one handful, in others sixty for one, and in still others thirty for one. He then explained the parable, showing that the seed was the word of his kingdom and that the word was to have different effects in the lives of those who heard it. Some hearts would be so hard they would not receive it at all, and the devil's cohorts would soon snatch it away. Others would receive it as a novelty as did the Athenians in Paul's day, but they would soon lose interest, particularly in face of persecution. The third class would consist of those who allow the word to be choked out by worldly concerns and their delight in riches. Only the fourth class was to be made up of those in whom the gospel would take root.

The parable means that only part of the preaching of the kingdom of God will bear fruit. The parable does away with the idea that the preaching of the gospel will be more and more effective and will inevitably bring a total triumph for the church as history progresses.

The second parable makes the point even more clearly. It is the story of the wheat and tares. Jesus said that a man went out to sow grain but that after he had done it an enemy came and sowed tares. The two kinds of plants grew up together, the one true wheat, the other plants that looked like wheat but were useless as food. In the story the servants wanted to pull up the tares, but the owner told them not to do that lest they uproot some of the wheat also. Instead they were to let both grow together until the harvest, when the grain would be gathered into the barns and the tares burned.

When Jesus was alone with his disciples he explained that the field was the world, the wheat represented those who belonged to him, and the tares were the children of the devil. Or, according to Jesus, the world would always contain within it those who were God's true children and those who were children of the devil. That would be true throughout church history. Moreover, since some of his children would look so much like those whom the devil counterfeited, no one was to try to separate the two on this earth lest some Christians should perish with the others. The point of the parable is that the unsatisfactory conditions will remain until the end of this age.

The other parables make similar points; that is, the extension of the kingdom of God will be accompanied by the devil's influence and will always be imperfect. It should be evident from the imperfect nature of the kingdom of God, as we see it today, that there is yet to be a kingdom in which the rule of the Lord Jesus Christ will be recognized. This is the third important point that must be stated about Christ's rule.

Christ told his disciples that there was to be a spiritual kingdom throughout the "church age." But he taught that there was to be a literal, future kingdom as well. In one parable he

compared himself to a nobleman who went into a far country
to receive a kingdom and then return. In the meantime he left
gifts in the hands of his servants, charging them to be faithful
and ready to give a good accounting at his return (Lk. 19:
11-27). On another occasion, after the resurrection, the disciples asked Jesus, "Lord, will you at this time restore the kingdom to Israel?" (Acts 1:6). He answered, "It is not for you to
know times or seasons which the Father has fixed by his own
authority [in other words, you are right about the fact of the
kingdom; but it is none of your business to know when]. But
you shall receive power when the Holy Spirit has come upon
you; and you shall be my witnesses in Jerusalem and in all
Judea and Samaria and to the end of the earth" (vv. 7-8).[4]

Imitators of Christ

For us the work of the kingdom of God falls in the last of those
statements. We are the witnesses, Christ's witnesses. We are to
bear the message of his rule throughout our cities, states, nations and the world.

As we do this we are to know that by the same exercise of
Christ's authority in the church we are uniquely equipped for
our task. He is our prophet, priest and king—and in a lesser
way we too are prophets, priests and kings. We are prophets
in the sense that we too are spokespersons for God in this
world. In Moses' day that was a fond wish only: "Would that
all the LORD's people were prophets!" (Num. 11:29). But in
our day, as a result of the outpouring of the Holy Spirit upon
the church at Pentecost, it has come true. Now, as Peter main-
tained, the words of the prophet Joel concerning the latter
days have been fulfilled. "This is what was spoken by the
prophet Joel: 'And in the last days it shall be, God declares,
that I will pour out my Spirit upon all flesh, and your sons
and your daughters shall prophesy, and your young men shall
see visions, and your old men shall dream dreams; yea, and
on my menservants and my maidservants in those days I will

pour out my Spirit; and they shall prophesy' " (Acts 2:16-18). As prophets we speak the Word of God to our contemporaries.

We are also priests. True, there will never be another priesthood like the Old Testament priesthood; Christ has perfected that forever. Yet there is a sense in which all God's people are priests. They all have access to God equally on the basis of Christ's sacrifice and are called upon to offer themselves to God in self-consecration, praise and service. Peter speaks of this explicitly, reminding us that we are "a holy priesthood, to offer spiritual sacrifices acceptable to God through Jesus Christ" (1 Pet. 2:5). Paul has the same idea in mind as he writes to the Romans. "I appeal to you therefore, brethren, by the mercies of God, to present your bodies as a living sacrifice, holy and acceptable to God, which is your spiritual worship" (Rom. 12:1). We are also to exercise our priesthood in intercessory prayer for one another and for the world.

Finally, there is a sense in which we are also kings with Christ. The book of Revelation says of the saints of God, "Thou ... hast made them a kingdom and priests to our God, and they shall reign on earth" (Rev. 5:10). How shall we reign? Not by lording it over one another, for that is not how Jesus exerts his reign among us. Rather, as the hymn says,

> *For not with swords' loud clashing,*
> *Nor roll of stirring drums,*
> *But deeds of love and mercy,*
> *The heavenly kingdom comes.*

Our kingship is expressed, not in privilege, but in responsibility.

13

QUENCHING GOD'S WRATH

To treat the work of the Lord Jesus Christ as prophet, priest and king has the advantage of appearing to cover his work in one manageable chapter. The disadvantage is that it does not adequately show how the various offices relate to one another nor indicate which office is most important. According to the Bible, Jesus' purpose was to die (Mk. 10:45).

That leads us to a further discussion of the meaning of his death. When we focus on his death, the problem of accepting it as the central aspect of his work is aggravated rather than decreased for contemporary people. The central biblical concepts for understanding the meaning of Christ's death are "propitiation" and "redemption," but each is difficult if not offensive to many. Propitiation deals with the idea of sacrifice, by which the wrath of God against sin is averted. Redemption refers to redeeming a slave from slavery. Neither of these seems compatible with the modern conception of what God does or should do. Can we believe that salvation is achieved by God's paying a price for our redemption? Doesn't that lead to those bizarre medieval ideas of Christ's becoming God's ransom price to the devil? As for propitiation, isn't the whole web of thought in which that idea operates outmoded? Can we really believe that wrath enters into the matter of salvation at all? Or if we can, how can it be that one man's death, however significant, can avert it?

Those are questions we must keep in mind as we begin to explore the matter of Christ's death. But we also want to ask, What exactly did the death of Christ accomplish? And how did it accomplish it? In answering these questions we want to look at the idea of propitiation in this chapter and at redemption in the next.

God Pacifying His Own Wrath

Propitiation is a little-understood concept in the biblical interpretation of Christ's death. We begin by noting that it has to do with sacrifices and that it refers to what Jesus accomplished in relation to God by his death. Redemption has to do with what he accomplished in relation to *us*. By redeeming us, Jesus freed *us* from the bondage of sin. In contrast, propitiation relates to *God* so that we can say: By his death Jesus propitiated the wrath of his Father against sin and thus made it possible for God to be propitious to his people.

But that requires explanation. In the first place, we need to note that the idea of propitiation presupposes the idea of the wrath of God. If God is not wrathful toward sin, there is no need to propitiate him and the meaning of the death of Christ must therefore be expressed in other categories. Right here many modern thinkers would stop, arguing that it is precisely for this reason that the term should not be used or, if it is used, that it should be given another meaning. "We can understand," such a person might say, "how the idea of propitiation would be appropriate in paganism where God was assumed to be capricious, easily offended and therefore often angry. But that is not the biblical picture of God. According to the Christian revelation, God is not angry. Rather, he is gracious and loving. It is not God who is separated from us because of sin, but rather we who are separated from God. Thus it is not God who is to be propitiated but we ourselves." Those who have argued this way have either rejected the idea of propitiation entirely, considering its presence in the Bible to be a carryover from paganism's imperfect way of thinking about God—or else they have interpreted the basic Greek word for propitiation to mean not Christ's propitiation of the wrath of God, but rather the covering over or expiation of our guilt by his sacrifice. In other words, they have regarded the work as directed toward man rather than toward God. A scholar who has led the way in this is the late C. H. Dodd of Cambridge, England, whose influence has led to the translation of the word "propitiation" as "expiation" in the relevant texts in the Revised Standard Version of the Bible (Rom. 3:25; Heb. 2:17; 1 Jn. 2:2; 4:10).[1]

At this point we must be appreciative of the work of those who have distinguished the pagan idea of propitiation from the Christian idea. For it is quite true that God is not capricious or easily angered, a God whom we must therefore propitiate in order to keep in his good graces. That is totally opposite to the Christian position, for God is quite correctly seen as a God of grace and love.

But that is not the whole of the matter, as sympathetic as one may be with the concerns of such scholars. First, we dare not forget what the Bible tells us about God's just wrath against sin, in accordance with which sin will be punished either in Christ or in the person of the sinner. We may feel, because of our particular cultural prejudices, that the wrath of God and the love of God are incompatible. But the Bible teaches that God is wrath and love at the same time. What is more, his wrath is not just a small and insignificant element that somehow is there alongside his far more significant and overwhelming love. Actually, God's wrath is a major element that may be traced all the way from God's judgment against sin in the garden of Eden to the final cataclysmic judgments recorded in the book of Revelation. (That emphasis has already been studied at considerable length in chapter seven.)

Second, although the word *propitiation* is used in biblical writings, it is not used in the same way as in pagan writings. In pagan rituals the sacrifice was the means by which people placated an offended deity. In Christianity it is never people who take the initiative or make the sacrifice, but God himself who out of his great love for sinners provides the way by which his wrath against sin may be averted. Moreover, he is himself the way—in Jesus. That is the true explanation of why God is never the explicit object of propitiation in the biblical writings. He is not mentioned as the object because he is also the subject, which is much more important. In other words, God himself placates his own wrath against sin so that his love may go out to embrace and save sinners.

The idea of propitiation is most clearly observed in the Old Testament sacrificial system, for if anything is conveyed through that system of sacrifices it is that God has himself provided the way by which a sinful man or woman may approach him. Sin means death, as was pointed out earlier. But the sacrifices teach that there is a way of escape and of approaching God. Another may die in a sinner's place. That may seem astounding, even (as some have wrongly suggested) immoral, but it is what the system of sacrifices teaches. Thus, the individual Israelite was instructed to bring an animal for sacrifice whenever he approached God; the family was to kill and consume an animal at the yearly observance of the Passover; the nation was to be thus represented by the high priest annually on the Day of Atonement when the blood of the offering was sprinkled upon the mercy seat of the ark of the covenant within the Holy of Holies of the Jewish temple. At the end of this process of instruction, Jesus appeared as the offering that was to take away "the sin of the world" (Jn. 1:29).

The progression is this: one sacrifice for one individual, one sacrifice for one family, one sacrifice for one nation, one sacrifice for the world. The way to God's presence is now open to anyone who will come, a fact symbolized by the rending of the veil of the temple (which separated the Holy of Holies from the rest of the temple) at Christ's death.

To Prove God's Righteousness

Only four New Testament texts actually use the word _propitiation,_ though the idea of sacrifice (to which it is linked) is dominant. The critical passage is Romans 3:23-26. "Since all have sinned and fall short of the glory of God, they are justified by his grace as a gift, through the redemption which is in Christ Jesus, whom God put forward as an expiation [propitiation] by his blood, to be received by faith. This was to show God's righteousness, because in his divine forbearance he had passed over former sins; it was to prove at the present time that he himself is righteous and that he justifies him who has faith in Jesus." How is propitiation to be taken in Paul's statement of the nature of Christ's work of atonement? Does it mean propitiation in the sense of the quieting of God's wrath against sin, or does it mean the covering over of guilt, the meaning reflected in the RSV translation?

If there were nothing but this passage to go on, those questions would perhaps be unanswerable. But we have the entire context of the opening section of Paul's letter. It is quite closely reasoned and has a direct bearing upon the nature of Christ's work stated here. We get the beginning of this context in the first chapter at verse 18, where Paul introduces his formal argument by the statement that "the wrath of God is revealed from heaven against . . . men who by their wickedness suppress the truth." The passage goes on to state that men and women have been given a knowledge of God in creation, including their own beings, but they have willfully turned away from this knowledge in order to reject God and set up a false and debased form of god in God's place. This is "ungodliness" and "wickedness." It is because of this that the wrath of God is directed against them. In the remainder of the chapter Paul shows how this works out. God has decreed that if they will not have him, they must have the result of their own debased thinking and living. Consequently, they are given over to a lie (so that their minds become darkened) and to depraved living, as a result of which envy, murder, strife, deceit, malignity, gossip, slander, hate and all kinds of other vices proliferate.

In the second chapter Paul moves from a discussion of the way in which the wrath of God works itself out in history to a discussion of its extent. He knows that women and men are often quite ready to accuse others while nevertheless excusing themselves. So he asks, "Is anyone exempt?" The answer is No. Thus, having shown how the wrath of God affects the pagan world (in chapter 1), he now shows that the so-called moral and religious people are affected too. Moral individuals are affected because, whatever they may imagine their own particular moral attainment to be, they nevertheless fall short of God's standard. What is more, they even boast in their supposed attainment and do not repent. They do not see that the grace and forbearance of God toward them are meant to lead them to repentance (2:4). Religious persons are also affected, for what they fail to see is that their valued religious practices clean up only the outside of their lives while leaving untouched the serious corruption within (2:28-29).

Paul's conclusion in chapter 3 is that all are under the wrath of God, for all have sinned. Nevertheless, at this point the righteousness and grace of God are revealed, for in the person of his Son Jesus Christ, God the Father has provided a way by which those who believe in him might be saved. Though we have sinned, we are nevertheless "justified by his grace as a gift, through the redemption which is in Christ Jesus, whom

God put forward as an expiation [propitiation] by his blood"
(3:24-25).

This means that the wrath of God directed against us because of our sin has now been quenched or turned aside by
God's action through the death of Christ. "The 'blood'—that
is, the sacrificial death—of Jesus Christ abolished God's anger
against us, and ensured that his treatment of us for ever after
would be propitious and favorable. Henceforth, instead of
showing himself to be against us, he would show himself in
our life and experience to be for us. What, then, does the
phrase 'a propitiation . . . by his blood' express? It expresses,
in the context of Paul's argument, precisely this thought: that
by his sacrificial death for our sins Christ pacified the wrath of God."[2]

The passage shows that the wrath of God, far from being
the capricious and conceited anger characteristic of the pagan
gods and which therefore does not need to be taken seriously
today, is actually the unyielding and terrifying opposition of
the holy God to all that is opposed to holiness. It is directed
against all, for all are unholy. At the same time, the passage
shows how God, out of that great love which is also a fundamental part of his nature, has himself acted to propitiate his
wrath and thereby save humanity.

The second New Testament passage to use the word *propitiation* is Hebrews 2:17. It does not have the same emphasis as
the text in Romans, for in Romans Paul is speaking explicitly
of the work of Christ in propitiating the wrath of God while in
Hebrews the author is concerned more with the *how* of propitiation, namely, with the kind of nature Christ needed to
have in order to make propitiation. His point is that Jesus became one with mankind in order to represent them as a faithful high priest. "Therefore he had to be made like his brethren in every respect, so that he might become a merciful and
faithful high priest in the service of God, to make expiation
[propitiation] for the sins of the people."

This text does not explicitly mention the wrath of God. But

it says nothing contrary to the idea of a propitiation of God's wrath against sin and, in fact, may even be said to suggest it, although indirectly. For example, the text speaks of Christ being a "merciful" priest. Mercy means to show favor to one who does not deserve it. So if those for whom Christ is a merciful priest do not deserve mercy, what they clearly deserve is God's wrath, which however has been turned away from them by Christ's sacrifice. The verse speaks of Christ being a priest "in the service of God" (literally, "in reference to those things which pertain to God"). So a work directed toward God rather than toward humanity is prominent. Finally, the passage also suggests the ancient sacrificial system. The author's reference to a "faithful high priest" is later explained in the categories of the priesthoods of Aaron and Melchizedek. Jesus is superior to those earlier priests because he offers the perfect and therefore final and all-inclusive sacrifice.

The last two uses of *propitiation* in the New Testament are in the First Epistle of John. "My little children, I am writing this to you so that you may not sin; but if any one does sin, we have an advocate with the Father, Jesus Christ the righteous; and he is the expiation [propitiation] for our sins, and not for ours only but also for the sins of the whole world" (2:1-2) and "In this is love, not that we loved God but that he loved us and sent his Son to be the expiation [propitiation] for our sins" (4:10).

What is the central concern of these verses? Again, neither speaks explicitly of God's wrath, but in the first verse the human dilemma is conveyed at least indirectly, just as in the verse from Hebrews. In this case, need is suggested by the reference to Jesus as our "advocate." Why do we need a lawyer or helper if, in fact, we do not stand in a position of difficulty before God? We are sinners, the point that John has been making in the preceding verses (1:5-10), and therefore we are not in good standing before God. Rather, we stand condemned and need an advocate. In this context it is understandable that John would choose a word that speaks of the work of a priest in turning away God's wrath, and bring this work forward as the sure ground by which we may approach God and be assured of his favor.

Another indication that this is what John is thinking about is his statement that Jesus' death for sins was "not for ours only but also for the sins of the whole world." It is likely that John is thinking of the fact that in Judaism the propitiatory sacrifice offered by the high priest on the Day of Atonement was for Jews only; now, since the death of Jesus, the sacrifice avails for Gentiles and Jews alike.

The final mention (1 Jn. 4:10) does not throw much light on the meaning of propitiation, but it does combine it with the idea of the love of God out of which the act of propitiation flows, thereby supplying us with "one of those resounding paradoxes which mean so much for the understanding of the Christian view of sacrifice."[3] Christ's death is a genuine propitiation of God's wrath. But paradoxically it is the love of God that makes the propitiation.

Here, then, we come to the heart of the gospel. In the act of propitiation we have the great good news that the one who is our Creator, but from whom we have turned in sin, is nevertheless at the same time our redeemer. Packer sums it up in this fashion:

> _The basic description of the saving death of Christ in the Bible is as a_ propitiation, _that is, as that which quenched God's wrath against us by obliterating our sins from his sight. God's wrath is his righteousness reacting against unrighteousness; it shows itself in retributive justice. But Jesus Christ has shielded us from the nightmare prospect of retributive justice by becoming our representative substitute, in obedience to his Father's will, and receiving the wages of sin in our place. By this means justice has been done, for the sins of all that will ever be pardoned were judged and punished in the person of God the Son, and it is on this basis that pardon is now offered to us offenders. Redeeming love and retributive justice joined hands, so to speak, at Calvary, for there God showed him-_

self to be "just, and the justifier of him that hath faith in Jesus."[4]

Light on Other Truths

The doctrine of Christ's sacrifice, conceived as a true propitiation of God's wrath against sin, is the heart of the gospel and throws valuable light on other doctrines. We may close this chapter by looking at some of them.

First, the nature of Christ's sacrifice throws light on *God's attributes*. It is customary in many contemporary theological circles to emphasize the love of God at the expense of his other attributes. We must not minimize the love of God, but we must maintain on the basis of the biblical revelation that love is not the only attribute of God or even, if we are looking at the matter in logical sequence, the first. Looked at in a logical sequence, the first attributes of God must be those that present him as the Creator and sustainer of this world: self-existence, self-sufficiency, eternity, sovereignty, holiness and omniscience. After them comes that attribute disclosed by the Fall and rebellion of the human race: wrath. Only then can we adequately talk about his love. God was love even before the Fall or, for that matter, from all eternity, but the full measure of that love is seen only in the offering up of Christ for us "while we were yet sinners" (Rom. 5:8).

So the fact of propitiation reminds us, first of all, that God is truly wrathful against sin as well as loving toward the sinner. Moreover, it enhances our appreciation of his love. Within this framework, the love of God is not merely some indulgent feeling of good will (which is what human love often is). It is rather an intense, demanding, holy love that is willing to pay the greatest price in order to save the one loved.

Second, the nature of Christ's sacrifice throws light on the nature of *the human dilemma*. If the coming of Christ is only an open declaration of God's favor toward women and men, a demonstration by which God seeks to capture our attention and win our love, then our condition as we stand in alienation from God is not serious. God loves us, whatever we may have done, and we may suppose that things will turn out all right in the end, whatever we may choose or not choose concerning Christ now. We do not have wrath to reckon with. However, if Christ's death is a propitiation of God's wrath, then the human situation is quite different. Wrath is real, and we may expect to feel the full force of that wrath unless we too become partakers in Christ's salvation.

The cross of Christ means, among other things, that our state is desperate, so desperate, in fact, that there is no hope for us except there. We are, as Paul says, "dead through ... trespasses and sins," prisoners of "the prince of the power of the air" and "by nature children of wrath, like the rest of mankind" (Eph. 2:1-3). These truths are taught so that men and women might turn, out of a sense of frightful spiritual danger, to the Savior.

Third, light is shed on the _person and work of Jesus Christ._ His nature as the God-man is illumined along the lines developed in chapter eleven. Only as one who is at the same time God and man can he make propitiation. His work is illumined in that this mission alone makes sense of what we find recorded about him in the Gospels.

To give just one example, we notice that in even the most dangerous situations he encountered—the hostility of raging mobs, temptation by Satan, the attempts at entrapment by those leaders of Israel who were antagonistic to him—Jesus was always in total and evident control. Yet as his death drew near, each of the Gospel writers tells us that he began to be greatly distressed and sorrowful (Mt. 26:37-38; Mk. 14:33-34; Lk. 22:44; Jn. 12:27), and three of them (Matthew, Mark and Luke) tell us that he prayed earnestly in the garden of Gethsemane that the cup which he was soon to drink might pass from him. What was that cup? Was it his physical death? If so, Jesus had less courage than did Socrates who faced his death with self-control and died calmly conversing of immortality. The only explanation other than the view that Jesus was a coward whose faith failed is that his death was quite different from that of the Athenian philosopher or our own. He was to die not only physically but also spiritually, thus being separated from God because of sin and thus bearing the wrath of God against sin on our behalf. The unique quality of his death was that on Calvary he experienced the horror of the wrath of God while making propitiation.

Fourth, the true *nature of the gospel* also emerges in this understanding of the death of Jesus. The gospel is not just a new possibility for achieving joy and fullness in this life, as some seem to suggest. It is not just a solution to what were previously troublesome and frustrating problems. It is rather something much deeper that has been done, something relating to God, on the basis of which and only on the basis of which these other blessings of salvation follow. "The gospel does bring us solutions to these problems, but it does so by first solving . . . the deepest of all human problems, the problem of man's relation with his Maker; and unless we make it plain that the solution of these former problems depends on the settling of this latter one, we are misrepresenting the message and becoming false witnesses of God."[5]

Finally, the nature of Christ's death as propitiation also has its bearing upon *Christian ethics*. Paul says, "The love of Christ controls us, because we are convinced that one has died for all; therefore all have died. And he died for all, that those who live might live no longer for themselves but for him who for their sake died and was raised" (2 Cor. 5:14-15). Or again, to refer to a text which more properly introduces the theme of the next chapter, "You are not your own; you were bought with a price. So glorify God in your body" (1 Cor. 6:19-20; compare 7:23). That God loved us so much that he sent his Son to bear his just wrath against sin in our place is the greatest and ultimately only adequate basis for Christian ethics. We love him because of his great love for us, and so we wish to serve him.

14

PAID
IN
FULL

Redemption and the work of the Lord as *redeemer* are among the most precious words in the Christian's vocabulary. They are not the terms most frequently used when we speak of Christ's work. We more often speak of him as Savior. We frequently refer to him as Lord. But they speak to us directly of what Jesus Christ did for our salvation and of what it cost him to do it.

In the early part of this century, B. B. Warfield delivered an address to incoming students in which he pointed out that the title redeemer conveys an intimate revelation. He wrote:

> *It gives expression not merely to our sense that we have received salvation from Him, but also to our appreciation of what it cost Him to procure this salvation for us. It is the name specifically of the Christ of the cross. Whenever we pronounce it, the cross is placarded before our eyes and our hearts are filled with loving remembrance not only that Christ has given us salvation, but that he paid a mighty price for it.*[1]

Warfield proved his assertion by a lengthy series of quotations from the hymns of the church in which the word *redeemer* occurs.

Let our whole soul an offering be
 To our Redeemer's Name.

While we pray for pardoning grace,
 Through our Redeemer's Name.

Almighty Son, Incarnate Word,
 Our Prophet, Priest, Redeemer, Lord.

O for a thousand tongues to sing
 My dear Redeemer's praise.

To our Redeemer's glorious Name
 Awake the sacred song.

All hail, Redeemer, hail,
 For thou hast died for me.

Guide where our infant Redeemer is laid.

My dear Redeemer and my Lord.

All glory, laud and honor
 To thee Redeemer, King.

Our blest Redeemer, ere he breathed
 His tender, last farewell.

Warfield cited at least double that number of hymns, and then did the same thing with hymns using the word *ransom,* which, he indicated, is a close synonym of redemption. Today, of course, such words are probably less loved than formerly. But that is because they are less understood and appreciated not because the idea behind the words is less attractive to Christians. Moreover, even if we admit that they have lost some of their popular appeal, they are more apt than many other words that describe what has been done for us in salvation.

The Salvation Triangle

We see this aptness when we consider the three major words relating to what happens in salvation: propitiation, justification and redemption. Each of these occurs in those key verses introducing the work of Christ in Paul's presentation of the gospel in the book of Romans: "They are justified by his grace as a gift, through the redemption which is in Christ Jesus, whom God put forward as an expiation [propitiation] by his blood, to be received by faith" (Rom. 3:24-25).

We can make the comparison easily in a triangle like the one shown below. The line connecting God the Father and Christians is justification. The arrow points downward, for justification refers to something God does to us. We are justified by grace on the basis of Christ's sacrifice. Propitiation is represented by the arrow that connects Christ with God the Father. This arrow points upward for Christ propitiated the Father by his death on our behalf. The third and bottom side of the triangle, the arrow connecting Jesus and ourselves is redemption.

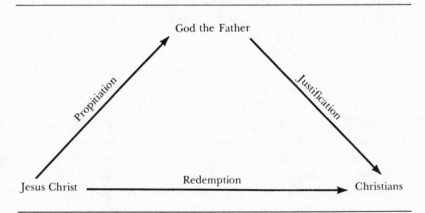

The Salvation Triangle

It points toward us, for redemption is something Jesus does for his people. He redeems us and sets us free.

In this diagram, God the Father is the initiator of one act: justification. Jesus is the initiator of two acts: propitiation directed toward the Father and redemption directed toward his people. We, who initiate nothing, receive both justification and redemption. But—and this is the point of the illustration —it is redemption alone of the three key words that actually describes what the Savior does for us in salvation. He redeems us! Therefore, it is natural that this word (or the idea it represents) should be most precious.

The Greek word at the base of the major word group meaning "redeem," "redeemer" and "redemption" is *luō*, which means "to loose" or "loosen." It was used of loosening clothes or unbinding armor. When applied to human beings it signified the loosing of bonds so that, for example, a prisoner became free. At times it was used of procuring the release of a prisoner by means of a ransom; in those cases it meant "to release by payment of a ransom price."

From this last use of the verb the noun *lutron* developed. It referred to the means by which the redemption of the prisoner was accomplished. It meant the "ransom price" itself. From this word a new verb developed, *lutroō*. Unlike the first verb, *luō*, which was merely a general term for "loosing" and would only occasionally mean "to ransom," this verb seems always to have meant "to release by payment of a price." From this, *lutrōsis* ("redemption," "liberation"), *apoluō* ("release," "set free," "divorce," "forgive") and other related terms were derived. Because prisoners were often slaves and slaves were, in effect, prisoners, these words also had to do with buying a slave with the intention of setting the purchased one free. In English something of these basic ideas is preserved in redeeming something from a pawn shop; the object is set free again by payment of its redemption price.

Thus far everything seems to be straightforward, for when

the word *redemption* is used of Christ's work it obviously means that work by which Jesus freed us from sin. But here problems develop. Just as some scholars have objected to the true meaning of propitiation, thinking that the idea of appeasing God's wrath is unworthy of the Christian God, some have also objected to this basic meaning of redemption. The idea of deliverance is all right to such people, but the idea of a ransom price is all wrong. "How can God extract a price for salvation?" they ask. "If Jesus had to pay the price of his death for our deliverance, doesn't that mean that God is actually selling his favors and that salvation is therefore no longer of grace?" In developing this objection, a serious attempt has been made in recent biblical scholarship to see the word *redemption* differently, generally as a word for "deliverance" but without the overtones of a ransom. Some of this work has been done by German scholars in whose language the word for redemption (*Erloesung*, but not *Loskaufung*) means deliverance only. English-speaking scholars also point out that the redemption word group does not always strictly involve the idea of a ransom price. For example, the Emmaus disciples speak of their shattered messianic expectations concerning Jesus by saying, "But we had hoped that he was the one to redeem Israel" (Lk. 24:21). They note that the disciples are not thinking of a ransome from sin or even of anything spiritual. They mean only that they had hoped that Jesus would have been the one to deliver them from Rome.

Such thinkers also point to verses that speak of a final redemption of our bodies. Luke 21:28—"When these things begin to take place, look up and raise your heads, because your redemption is drawing near." Romans 8:23—"And not only the creation, but we ourselves, who have the first fruits of the Spirit, groan inwardly as we wait for adoption as sons, the redemption of our bodies." Ephesians 4:30—"And do not grieve the Holy Spirit of God, in whom you were sealed for the day of redemption."

What can be said to this objection? An immediate answer is that the Emmaus disciples obviously misunderstood the kind of redemption Jesus came to bring. Another is that, as in the case of propitiation, the price paid is not really a price paid by another to God but rather a price God pays to himself. It is God paying our bill so that salvation for us might be truly free. A third answer is that there certainly is a sense in which our ultimate redemption is a deliverance from this sinful world. A full answer, however, involves a complete study of the lexical data. There are four areas.

First, the New Testament ideas of redemption are necessarily conditioned by Old Testament forms; in the Old Testament the idea of a ransom or ransom price is prominent. In the Old Testament background three words are particularly significant. The first is *gaal* ("to set free") or *goel* (usually translated "kinsman redeemer"). It refers to the duty incumbent upon a relative to help some member of his family in preserving his family's honor or possessions. For example, if a man should lose his property through debt, as was the case with Naomi's husband as told in the book of Ruth, it was the duty of the kinsman redeemer (in that case, Boaz) to buy the property back—thereby restoring it to the family name. That duty would also extend to buying one of the family out of slavery (Lev. 25:47-55).

The second word is *padah*. It means "to ransom by paying a price," as in the redemption of the first-born, which otherwise would belong to the Lord (Ex. 13:11-14; Num. 18:15-16). It differs from *gaal* in that the redemption to which it refers is voluntary rather than obligatory as in the case of a kinsman.

The third word is *kopher* which means "a ransom price." Suppose, for example, that an ox had gored somebody to death. That was a crime as a result of which the ox could be killed or in certain circumstances (if there was negligence) the owner of the ox could be killed. He would have to forfeit his life for the one whose life had been taken. But he could redeem his life by *kopher*. That means that, if he could fix a price settled on by the relatives of the one who had been killed, the price would stand in place of the forfeiture of his life (Ex. 21: 28-32).

These three words, each with its connotations and laws, indicate that the idea of redemption by payment of a price was not only common but actually a fundamental principle in the social and religious life of Israel. Unless it can be demonstrated otherwise, redemption rather than the more limited idea of deliverance should be the underlying New Testament conception.

Second, the words for redemption also occur with the idea of the payment of a ransom price in secular Greek of the New Testament period, largely in reference to the redemption of prisoners of war or slaves. In that case, the price is so prominent that it is even stated in standard formulas of manumission. For example, "____ sold to the Pythian Apollo a male slave named ____ at a price of ____ minae, on the condition that he shall be set free."[2]

Third, the most important New Testament passages, those that use the redemption vocabulary of Christ's work, almost always stress the price paid for our deliverance. Matthew 20: 28 says, "The Son of man came not to be served but to serve, and to give his life as a ransom for many." Here the price of redemption is stated by the Lord himself; it is his life. Titus 2:14 speaks of Jesus "who gave himself for us to redeem us from all iniquity and to purify for himself a people of his own who are zealous for good deeds." The use of sacrificial terminology in this verse ("iniquity" and "purify") indicates that the author is not thinking of Christ's gift of himself as a living gift merely, as in service, but rather as a gift of himself in death. So again the price of Christ's life is prominent. Finally, in 1 Peter 1:18-19 the clearest language of all is employed. "You know that you were ransomed from the futile ways inherited from your fathers, not with perishable things such as silver and gold, but with the precious blood of Christ, like that of a lamb without blemish or spot." In each of these (and in other passages) redemption is accomplished by payment of the greatest price that could possibly be imagined, namely, the death or blood of Jesus Christ, the Son of God.

The fourth line of support for the traditional meaning of redemption is that the most common words for redemption, the ones we have been studying, are not the only words for it occurring in the New Testament. On the contrary, there are two others, each of which also involves the idea of deliverance by payment of a price. The idea is inherent in the very meaning of the words themselves. The first is *agorazō*. It means "to buy" and occurs in verses like 1 Corinthians 6:19-20; 7:22-23; 2 Peter 2:1; Revelation 5:9-10; all speak of the chosen of God being purchased by the death of Christ. The second word is *exagorazō,* which is based upon the former word and means "to buy out." Since both are closely related to the word *agora,* which means the marketplace or place of business, these words really mean "to buy out of the marketplace," so that the one who has been purchased might never return there again.

Slaves to Sin

A lexical study of the word *redeem* does not really give us its full theological meaning, however, so we now turn to three crucial doctrines basic to it.

The first doctrine is that of man's original state, which was sinless. In that state the first man and woman were free, with a freedom proper to created beings. They were in fellowship with God. Redemption implies that one must be bought back to enjoy that state that has been enjoyed previously. Here, of course, Christianity runs counter to the dominant view of man in our day: that he is gradually working his way upward from a less perfect or even an impersonal beginning.[3] In the popular contemporary view there is no guilt. That is why it is popular. On the contrary, the human race is to be praised and is in fact its own savior. The biblical view, embodied in the word _redemption_ as well as in other terms, is that we are actually fallen from a better state and therefore are guilty and need a Savior. In fact, so great is our guilt and so deep our Fall that no one but God can save us.

The second major doctrine related to the biblical idea of redemption is the Fall, which has already been suggested. There is a parallel between the ways in which a person could fall into slavery in antiquity and how a person is said to be bound by sin in the Bible. In the ancient world there were three ways in which a person could become a slave. First, one could be born into slavery. That is, if a person's father and mother were slaves, that person became a slave as well. Second, a person could fall into slavery through conquest. Thus, if one city or state overcame another city or state in warfare, the defeated inhabitants might be led into captivity. Third, a person could become a slave through debt. If he or she owed more than could be paid back, it was possible for that person to be sold into slavery in order to discharge the debt.

These ways of falling into slavery seem to correspond with the various ways in which the Bible speaks of sin having a hold over the individual. One could be born a slave in antiquity. In the same way the Bible speaks of all since Adam being born into sin. David wrote, "Behold, I was brought forth in iniquity, and in sin did my mother conceive me" (Ps. 51:5). David does not mean that his mother was living in sin when she conceived him or that there was something sinful or wrong about the act of conception itself. He means that there was never a moment in his existence that he was free from sin and that he inherited that sinful nature from his parents as they had from their parents before them. Again, one could become a slave through conquest, and the Bible speaks of sin having dominion over a person. David wrote of "presumptuous sins" and prayed that they might not have "dominion" over him (Ps. 19:13). The final possibility, that of becoming a slave through debt, is suggested by Romans 6:23, which speaks of "the wages of sin" as death. The expression does not mean that sin is rewarded, except in an ironical sense. It means that sin is indebtedness and that only the death of the sinner can pay the bill.

The Price of Freedom

The ideas of an original or perfect state and a subsequent Fall are important to the concept of redemption, but they are still not the central idea. The heart of the matter is that, although we have fallen into desperate slavery through sin and are held by it as by a cruel tyrant, Christ has nevertheless purchased our freedom from sin by his blood. He paid the price in order that we might be set free.

Perhaps the greatest biblical illustration of salvation (and what is meant by redemption particularly) is the story of Hosea. Hosea was a minor prophet—minor in regard to length, not importance—whose writing is based upon the story of his marriage. It was an unfortunate marriage from a human viewpoint, for his wife proved unfaithful to him. But it was a special marriage from God's viewpoint. God had told Hosea that the marriage would work out in that fashion but he nevertheless asked Hosea to go through with it in order to provide an illustration of God's love. God loved the people whom he had taken to himself even when they proved unfaithful by committing spiritual adultery with the world and its values. The marriage was to be a pageant. Hosea was to play the part of God. His wife would play the part of unfaithful Israel. She would be unfaithful, but the wilder she got, the more Hosea would love her. That is the way God loves us even when we run away from him and dishonor him.

Hosea describes his commission by saying, "When the LORD first spoke through Hosea, the LORD said to Hosea, 'Go, take to yourself a wife of harlotry and have children of harlotry, for the land commits great harlotry by forsaking the LORD.' So

_ Paid in Full 205_

he went and took Gomer the daughter of Diblaim, and she conceived and bore him a son" (Hos. 1:2-3).

There are significant lessons in the early stages of this drama—in the naming of the children born to Hosea and Gomer and in Hosea's care for his wife even after she had left him—but the climax comes at the point at which Gomer fell into slavery, probably because of debt. Hosea was told to buy her back as a demonstration of the way in which the faithful God loves and saves his people. Slaves were always sold naked in the ancient world, and that would have been true of Gomer as she was put up on the auction block in the capital city. She had apparently been a beautiful woman. She was still beautiful even in her fallen state. So when the bidding started the offers were high, as the men of the city bid for the body of the female slave.

"Twelve pieces of silver," said one.

"Thirteen," said Hosea.

"Fourteen."

"Fifteen," said Hosea.

The low bidders dropped out. But someone added, "Fifteen pieces of silver and a bushel of barley."

"Fifteen pieces of silver and a bushel and a half of barley," said Hosea.

The auctioneer must have looked around for a higher bid and seeing none said, "Sold to Hosea for fifteen pieces of silver and a bushel and a half of barley." Now Hosea owned his wife. He could have killed her if he wished. He could have made a public spectacle of her in any way he might have chosen. But instead, he put her clothes back on her, led her away into the anonymity of the crowd, and demanded love of her while nevertheless promising the same from himself.

Here is the way he tells it: "And the LORD said to me, 'Go again, love a woman who is beloved of a paramour and is an adulteress; even as the LORD loves the people of Israel,though they turn to other gods and love cakes of raisins.' So I bought her for fifteen shekels of silver and a homer and a lethech of barley. And I said to her, 'You must dwell as mine for many days; you shall not play the harlot, or belong to another man; so will I also be to you' " (Hos. 3:1-3). Hosea had a right to demand what she had formerly been unwilling to give, but as he demands it he promises love from himself. The point of the story is that God thus loves all who are his true spiritual children.

This is what redemption means: to buy out of slavery. If we understand Hosea's story, we understand that we are the slave sold on the auction block of sin. We were created for intimate fellowship with God and for freedom, but we have disgraced ourselves by unfaithfulness. First we have flirted with and then committed adultery with this sinful world and its values. The world has even bid for our soul, offering sex, money, fame, power and all the other items in which it traffics. But Jesus, our faithful bridegroom and lover, entered the marketplace to buy us back. He bid his own blood. There is no higher bid than that. And we became his. He reclothed us, not in the wretched rags of our old unrighteousness, but in his new robes of righteousness. He has said to us, "You must dwell as mine . . . ; you shall not . . . belong to another . . . ; so will I also be to you."

Free to Serve

Redemption has two consequences. First, it means we are free. Paradoxical as it may sound, to be purchased by Jesus is to be set free—free from the guilt and tyranny of the law and from sin's power. Paul speaks of this freedom at the high point of the book of Galatians where he challenges those to whom he is writing. "For freedom Christ has set us free; stand fast therefore, and do not submit again to a yoke of slavery" (Gal. 5:1).

Yet this is a special kind of freedom. It does not mean that we are set free to do anything we might wish, to sin with impunity or once again fall back into the bondage of rebellion and unfaithfulness. We are released to serve God. We are set free to will the good. We are delivered in order that we might obey and love Jesus. As Paul writes: "You are not your own; you were bought with a price. So glorify God in your body" (1 Cor. 6:19-20). Redemption is a glorious thing. Thoughts of it should warm our hearts and lift us up in praise to that one who gave himself that we might be free. But it is not only that. It also calls upon us to make the highest possible level of commitment. Just as Jesus gave himself for us, so also must we give ourselves for him. We must be willing, eager and determined to serve him. He died for us because of his great love. That love, an amazing love, "demands my soul, my life, my all."

THE GREATNESS OF GOD'S LOVE

15

Several years before his death the Swiss theologian Karl Barth came to the United States for a series of lectures. At one of these, after a very impressive lecture, a student asked a typically American question. He said, "Dr. Barth, what is the greatest thought that has ever passed through your mind?" The aging professor paused for a long time as he obviously thought about his answer. Then he said with great simplicity:

Jesus loves me! This I know,
For the Bible tells me so.

If the love of God is the greatest thing in the universe, why have we left a discussion of it until now? Why didn't we begin with it, and then place God's other attributes in perspective? Why are we discussing it in volume two of this four-volume series, rather than in volume one which more particularly dealt with God's attributes? The answer is that, although God's love is indeed important and great, we cannot really understand or appreciate it in our fallen state until we know some other things about him and about ourselves. These things must necessarily be in something like a sequence: first, our creation in God's image; second, our sin; third, the revelation of the wrath of God against us because of our sin; and fourth, redemption. If we do not have the sequence firmly in mind, we are unable to appreciate (let alone marvel at) God's love as we should. Instead, it might seem only reasonable that God should love us. "After all, we are really quite lovable," we think. However, when we see ourselves as standing in violation of the just law of God and under God's wrath, then to know that God loves us is truly remarkable. Paul makes this emphasis when he writes, "But God shows his love for us in that while we were yet sinners Christ died for us" (Rom. 5:8).

That leads us to another reason why we have not been able to look at the love of God earlier. The love of God is seen in its fullness only at the cross of Jesus Christ. The intimations of God's love in creation and providence are somewhat ambiguous. There are earthquakes as well as beautiful sunsets, cancer and other forms of sickness as well as health. Only at the cross does God show his love fully and without ambiguity.

For that reason it is difficult to find a verse in the New Testament that speaks about God's love without also speaking in the same verse or in the immediate context about God's gift of his Son on Calvary. John 3:16—"For God so loved the world that he gave his only Son, that whoever believes in him should not perish but have eternal life." Galatians 2:20—"I have been crucified with Christ; it is no longer I who live, but Christ who lives in me; and the life I now live in the flesh I live by faith in the Son of God, who loved me and gave himself for me." 1 John 4:10—"In this is love, not that we loved God but that he loved us and sent his Son to be the expiation [propitiation] for our sins." Revelation 1:5—"To him who loves us and has freed us from our sins by his blood." Such verses hold the love of God and the cross of Christ together. What is more, they are among the most important texts on both subjects.

Only after we have come to appreciate the meaning of the

cross can we appreciate the love behind it. Seeing this, Augustine once called the cross "a pulpit" from which Christ preached God's love to the world.

Love Behind

When we say we can appreciate the love of God in its fullness only after we have come to understand the doctrines of creation, sin, wrath and redemption—that is, only when we stand on the Easter side of the cross—we must be careful. For the love of God does not originate there but rather is prior to and greater than each of those subsequent matters. If we fail to see that, we are likely to imagine that once God was wrathful toward us but now, since Christ died, his wrath has somehow been changed to love. That is wrong, and it distorts the meaning of the cross.

The love of God stands behind everything: behind creation, behind Christ's death, even (though it is difficult to understand this) behind his wrath toward sin. How can God love us prior to and in greater measure than his wrath toward us and still be wrathful toward us? Augustine said that God hated us "in so far as we were not what he himself had made," while nevertheless loving what he had made and would make of us again.[1] We are reconciled to God, not because Christ's death somehow changed God's attitude toward us, but because God's love sent Christ to make the way by which sin, which bars us from a realization of his love, might be removed forever.

C. S. Lewis captures this idea neatly toward the end of his treatise on *The Four Loves*.

> We must not begin with mysticism, with the creature's love for God, or with the wonderful foretastes of the fruition of God vouchsafed to some in their earthly life. We begin at the real beginning, with love as the Divine energy. . . . God, who needs nothing, loves into existence wholly superfluous creatures in order that he may love and perfect them. He creates the universe, already foreseeing—or should

*we say "seeing"? there are no tenses in God–the buzzing cloud of
flies about the cross, the flayed back pressed against the uneven
stake, the nails driven through the mesial nerves, the repeated in-
cipient suffocation as the body drops, the repeated torture of back
and arms as it is time after time, for breath's sake, hitched up. If
I may dare the biological image, God is a "host" who deliberately
creates his own parasites; causes us to be that we may exploit and
"take advantage of" him.* [2]

Wrath has intervened to hide the love of God from us, but
when wrath is removed we see his prior love and are drawn
to God by it.

A New Word

What can we say about the love of God for his creatures, a love
out of which they are not only created and redeemed but also
preserved for an eternity of fellowship with him? Obviously,
nothing we could say could exhaust the full measure of his
love. God's love is always infinitely deeper than our awareness
or expression of it.

The Bible is simple when it speaks about God's love, and
one of the simple things it says is that God's love is *great.* "But
God, who is rich in mercy, out of the great love with which he
loved us . . ." (Eph. 2:4). John 3:16 implies as much by the little
word *so:* "For God so loved the world that . . ." It means, "God
loved the world so greatly that . . ." Of course, when God says
that his love is great he is not using the word as we do when
we say that some relatively normal thing is great—a great
concert, a great dinner or something similar. God is a master
of understatement. So when he says that his love is great he is
really saying that his love is so stupendous that it goes far beyond our own ideas of greatness or our own understanding.

A person once captured the idea on a card on which he had
had John 3:16 printed. The verse was arranged in such a way
that the greatness of each part of the verse was evident. It
looked like this:

God	*the greatest Lover*
so loved	*the greatest degree*
the world	*the greatest company*
that he gave	*the greatest act*
his only begotten Son,	*the greatest gift*
that whosoever	*the greatest opportunity*
believeth	*the greatest simplicity*
in him	*the greatest attraction*
should not perish,	*the greatest promise*
but	*the greatest difference*
have	*the greatest certainty*
everlasting life.	*the greatest possession*

Over it all was the title, "Christ—the Greatest Gift."

An even better way of acknowledging the greatness of the love of God is to notice that the biblical writers probably invented, or at least raised to entirely new levels, a brand new word for love—so real was their need for a superlative word to express the unique love they had discovered through the biblical revelation.

The Greek language is a language rich in words for *love*. The first of the ancient Greek words was *storgē*. It referred to a kind of general affection, particularly within the family. The closest English equivalent would be "fondness." The Greek would say, "I love [am fond of] my children."

The second of the Greek words is *philia* from which we get the English words *philanthropy* and *Philadelphia*. It refers to friendship. Jesus used this word when he said that the person "who loves father or mother more than me is not worthy of me" (Mt. 10:37).

The third Greek word is *eros,* the word for sensual love. From it we get our English word *erotic.* This type of love had become so debased by New Testament times that the word is never used in the Bible, even though the biblical writers spoke approvingly of sexual love.

Yet when the Hebrew Old Testament was translated into

Greek and when the New Testament writers wrote in Greek, they found none of these common words adequate for conveying the true biblical conceptions. They took another word entirely, one without strong associatons, and used it almost exclusively. It had been little used previously. So they were able to infuse it with an entirely new character. By doing so they created a word that in time came to convey the type of love they wanted: *agapē*.

It was vague, but it could be and in fact was made to convey the right ideas. Does God love with a righteous, holy love? Yes. That love is *agapē*. Is God's love gracious, sovereign, everlasting? Yes, that too. "I have loved you with an everlasting love," God told Jeremiah (Jer. 31:3). That love is *agapē*. Thus *agapē* became the supreme word for speaking about God's love, a new love revealed initially by God through Judaism and then disclosed in its fullness in Jesus Christ through biblical Christianity.

Oceans Drained
Second, the Bible teaches that God's love is infinite. This is not the same as saying that God's love is great; the distinguishing mark is its inexpendability. It cannot be exhausted, nor even fully understood. Paul captures this idea when he prays that those to whom he is writing "may have power to comprehend with all the saints what is the breadth and length and height and depth, and to know the love of Christ which surpasses knowledge, that you may be filled with all the fulness of God" (Eph. 3:18-19). Logically analyzed, his words are contradictory; Paul's prayer is that the Christians might know the unknowable. That is Paul's way of emphasizing that he wants them to enter more deeply into the knowledge of God's infinite love.

How can we comprehend the infinite love of God? We can know it, but only in part. We have been touched by it, yet its fullness lies forever beyond us—just as the infinity of the universe lies beyond the probing human eye.

One hymn puts this aspect of God's love in memorable language. It was written by F.M. Lehman, but the final stanza (perhaps the best) was added to it later after it was found written on the wall of a room in an asylum by a man said to be insane but who had obviously come to know God's love.

> *The love of God is greater far*
> > *Than tongue or pen can ever tell;*
> *It goes beyond the highest star,*
> > *And reaches to the lowest hell.*
> *The guilty pair, bowed down with care,*
> > *God gave his Son to win:*
> *His erring child he reconciled,*
> > *And rescued from his sin.*
>
> *Oh, love of God, how rich and pure!*
> > *How measureless and strong!*
> *It shall forevermore endure—*
> > *The saints' and angels' song.*
>
> *Could we with ink the ocean fill,*
> > *And were the skies of parchment made;*
> *Were every stalk on earth a quill,*
> > *And every man a scribe by trade;*
> *To write the love of God above*
> > *Would drain the oceans dry;*
> *Nor could the scroll contain the whole,*
> > *Though stretched from sky to sky.*

This is the song of everyone who through Jesus Christ has come to know the infinite love of God.

Gift-Love

Third, God also tells us that his love is a *giving* love. That is the heart of John 3:16. "God so loved the world that he gave his only Son." It is in the nature of God's love to give, and when he gives it is not just a trifle but rather the very best. In *The Four Loves,* C. S. Lewis distinguishes between Gift-love and Need-love, pointing out that it is the former, Gift-love, that characterizes the love of God the Father. "Divine Love is Gift-love. The Father gives all he is and has to the Son. The Son gives Himself back to the Father, and gives Himself to the world, and for the world to the Father, and thus the world (in Himself) back to the Father too."[3] Nowhere is this better seen than in the gift of Jesus for our salvation.

There are two senses in which the Gift-love of the Father is seen in Jesus' death. First, Jesus is the best God had to give, for there is no one to compare with God's Son. Second, in giving Jesus, God gave himself, and there is nothing that anyone can give greater than that.

A minister was once talking to a couple who were having difficulties in their marriage. There was much bitterness and pain, coupled with an acute lack of understanding. At one point in the exchange the husband spoke up in obvious exasperation. "I've given you everything," he said to his wife. "I've given you a new home. I've given you a new car and all the clothes you can wear. I've given you . . ." The list went on.

When he had ended, the wife said sadly, "That much is true, John. You have given me everything . . . but yourself."

The greatest gift that anyone can give is himself or herself, and apart from that gift all other gifts are relatively insignificant. God gave himself in Jesus.

Choosing Love

Fourth, God's love is a *sovereign* love. Because God is God and is therefore under obligation to nobody, he is free to love whom he chooses. Indeed, he declares as much, saying, "Jacob I loved, but Esau I hated" (Rom. 9:13). Or again, in reference to Israel, "It was not because you were more in number than any other people that the LORD set his love upon you and chose you, for you were the fewest of all peoples; but it is because the LORD loves you, and is keeping the oath which he swore to your fathers" (Deut. 7:7-8).

If God is sovereign in his love, it means that his love is un-influenced by anything in the creature. And if that is so, it is the same as saying that the cause of God's love lies only in him-self. He loves whom he pleases. That is clear in both texts cited in the preceding paragraph. Thus the point of the reference to Jacob and Esau is not that Jacob was more lovable and that God therefore loved him rather than his brother, but rather that God set his love upon Jacob purely as an act of his sov-ereign will. He made that clear by choosing Jacob over Esau before the twins were born and thus before they had a chance to do anything either good or evil. Similarly, the verse from Deuteronomy explicitly denies that God loved Israel because of anything in them, such as their strength or size as a nation (they were not large as nations go). Rather it affirms that God loved them because he loved them.

To most people this is an unpopular teaching, but it is the only way things can be if God is truly to be God. Assume the opposite: God's love is regulated by something other than his sovereignty. In that case God would be regulated by this other thing (whatever it is) and would thus be brought under its power. That is impossible if he is still to be God. In Scrip-ture no cause for God's love other than his electing is ever given. It is always that "he destined us in love to be his sons through Jesus Christ, _according to the purpose of his will,_ to the praise of his glorious grace which he freely bestowed on us in the Beloved" (Eph. 1:5-6).

A second principle related to the sovereign character of God's love is no less important. It is that God's love is extended toward individuals. It is not a general good will directed toward everyone en masse and hence toward no one in par-ticular, but rather a love that singles out individuals and blesses them specifically and abundantly. "God's purpose of love, formed before creation (cf. Eph. 1:4), involved, first, the choice and selection of those whom he would bless and, second, the appointment of the benefits to be given them and the means whereby these benefits would be procured and enjoyed....The exercise of God's love towards individual sinners in time is the execution of a purpose to bless those same individual sinners which he formed in eternity."[4]

For Time and Eternity

A fifth and final point about the love of God is that it is *eternal.* Just as its origins are to be found in eternity past, so is its end to be found in eternity future. In other words, it has no end at all. Paul writes: "Who shall separate us from the love of Christ? Shall tribulation, or distress, or persecution, or famine, or nakedness, or peril, or sword? As it is written, 'For thy sake we are being killed all the day long; we are regarded as sheep to be slaughtered.' No, in all these things we are more than conquerors through him who loved us. For I am sure that neither death, nor life, nor angels, nor principalities, nor things present, nor things to come, nor powers, nor height, nor depth, nor anything else in all creation, will be able to separate us from the love of God in Christ Jesus our Lord" (Rom. 8: 35-39).

There are two classes of possible "separators" in Paul's list of the many potential threats to a Christian's relationship to God's love, and he denies the effectiveness of both of them. The first class concerns our natural enemies as persons living in an imperfect and ungodly world: poverty, hunger, natural disasters and persecutors. These cannot separate. As we read the list and think over Paul's experiences as a minister of the gospel, we realize that these words of assurance were not said lightly. Paul had himself endured these enemies (2 Cor. 6: 5-10; 11:24-33). Yet they had not separated him from the love of God, which is eternal. Nor will they separate us if we should have to undergo such suffering.

The second class of enemies is supernatural or, as we might

prefer to say, in the very nature of things. Here Paul lists death, life, angels, demonic powers, and anything else that may be assumed to fall within this category. Can they separate us from God's love? Paul answers that these cannot separate us either, for God is greater than any of them.

There is one last point. As Paul gets to the end of his statement of the everlasting and victorious character of God's love, he reaches the high point of this Epistle. He speaks of "the love of God [which is] *in Christ Jesus.*" This brings us back to the point with which we began, that of God's love being seen at the cross. But there is this additional thought: we must not only look to Christ in the sense of seeing the love of God displayed in him but must actually be "in him" in the sense of a personal relationship to him by faith, if we would know that love. So the question is: Do we thus know him? Have we found the great love of God to be a love for us through faith in Christ's sacrifice? Are we his? Is Jesus our own personal Savior and Lord?

There is no other way to know the love of God personally; therefore there is really no other way to know the love of God at all. It must begin by our commitment to Christ. God has decreed that it is only in Christ that his great, infinite, giving, sovereign and eternal love for sinners may be known.

16

THE PIVOTAL DOCTRINE: RESURRECTION

Which is more important to Christian theology: the death of Jesus Christ or his resurrection? The question is unanswerable. Although the death of Christ is what he explicitly came into the world to accomplish, the resurrection is no less important historically as evidence for Christ's claims. It is only because of the resurrection that the gospel of the cross was understood and then was preserved and transmitted across the centuries to us.

The significance of the resurrection is seen from the first moments of the Christian era. To a degree the disciples had believed in Christ prior to his death and resurrection. An example of their immature but genuine faith is Peter's testimony: "You are the Christ, the Son of the living God" (Mt. 16:16). But their faith was profoundly shaken by the crucifixion, so much so that his followers immediately began to scatter back to where they had come from. And Peter, who had given that remarkable testimony, denied the Lord three times on the night of Christ's arrest, even before the crucifixion. These men and women had believed, but the arrest and crucifixion buried their belief. Yet within three days, after the resurrection, their faith had again sprung forth, and they went out to present the gospel of the crucified but risen Savior to the world.

The death and resurrection of Jesus were the core of their message. Jesus had himself shown the way on the evening of his resurrection when he taught his scattering disciples out of the Old Testament. "Then he opened their minds to understand the scriptures, and said to them, 'Thus it is written, that the Christ should suffer and on the third day rise from the dead, and that repentance and forgiveness of sins should be preached in his name to all nations, beginning from Jerusalem. You are witnesses of these things' " (Lk. 24:45-48). Later Paul described the nature of that very early form of the apostles' preaching, saying that he had delivered to the Corinthians only what he himself had received, "that Christ died for our sins in accordance with the scriptures, that he was buried, that he was raised on the third day in accordance with the scriptures, and that he appeared to Cephas, then to the twelve. Then he appeared to more than five hundred brethren at one time, most of whom are still alive, though some have fallen asleep. Then he appeared to James, then to all the apostles. Last of all, as to one untimely born, he appeared also to me" (1 Cor. 15:3-8). Peter preached that David had written of Christ's resurrection. "For thou wilt not abandon my soul to Hades, nor let thy Holy One see corruption" (Acts 2:27, from Ps. 16:10). The other New Testament preachers did likewise. As many contemporary students of the earliest preaching have noted, the death and resurrection of Christ were always at the heart of the apostles' preaching.[1]

The resurrection proved that Jesus Christ is who he claimed to be and that he accomplished what he claimed to have come to earth to accomplish. Evangelist Reuben A. Torrey called the resurrection of Jesus Christ "the Gibraltar of Christian evidences, the Waterloo of infidelity." The resurrection is the historical base upon which all other Christian doctrines are built and before which all honest doubt must falter.

If it can be shown that Jesus of Nazareth actually rose from the dead, as the early Christians believed and as the Scriptures claim, then the Christian faith rests upon an impregnable foundation. If it stands, the other doctrines stand. On the other hand, if the resurrection falls, the other truths fall also. Thus the apostle Paul wrote: "If Christ has not been raised, then our preaching is in vain and your faith is in vain. We are even found to be misrepresenting God, because we testified of God that he raised Christ, whom he did not raise if it is true that the dead are not raised. For if the dead are not raised, then Christ has not been raised. If Christ has not been raised, your faith is futile and you are still in your sins. Then those also who have fallen asleep in Christ have perished" (1 Cor. 15:14-18).

The Sign of Jonah

What doctrines stand with the resurrection? The first is that there is a God and that the God of the Bible is the true God. Is there a God? If so, what kind of God is he? These are the first and most important questions that any religion or religious teacher must answer. But very different answers have been given to such questions by religious teachers. How can we be sure which of those answers are right, if any? The resurrection of Jesus Christ alone gives certainty.

Every effect must have an adequate cause . . . and the only cause adequate to account for the Resurrection of Christ is God, the God of the Bible. While here on earth, as everyone who has carefully read the story of His life knows, our Lord Jesus went up and down the land proclaiming God, the God of the Bible, the God of Abraham, Isaac and Jacob as He loved to call Him, the God of the Old Testament as well as the New. He said that men would put Him

to death, that they would put Him to death by crucifixion, and He
gave many details as to what the manner of His death would be.
He further said that after His body had been in the grave three days
and three nights, God, the God of Abraham, the God of Isaac and
the God of Jacob, the God of the Bible, the God of the Old Testa-
ment as well as the God of the New Testament, would raise Him
from the dead. This was a great claim to make. It was an apparent-
ly impossible claim. For centuries men had come and men had gone,
men had lived and men had died and as far as human knowledge
founded upon definite observation and experience was concerned,
that was the end of them. But this man Jesus does not hesitate to
claim that His experience will be directly contrary to the uniform
experience of long, long centuries. . . .

That was certainly an acid test of the existence of the God He
preached, and His God stood the test. He did exactly the apparently
impossible thing that our Lord Jesus said he would do. . . . The
fact that Jesus was thus miraculously raised makes it certain that
the God who did it really exists and that the God He preached is
the true God.[2]

Second, the resurrection of Jesus Christ establishes the doctrine of our Lord's deity. When he lived upon earth Jesus
claimed to be equal with God and that God would raise him
from the dead three days after his execution by the Jewish
and Roman authorities. If he was wrong in that, his claim was
either the raving of a deranged man or blasphemy. If he was
right, the resurrection would be God's way of substantiating
that claim. Did he substantiate it? Did Jesus rise from the
dead? Yes, he did. The resurrection is God's seal on Christ's
claim to divinity.

Paul, who knew that Jesus had been raised, writes that
Jesus was "designated Son of God in power according to the
Spirit of holiness by his resurrection from the dead" (Rom.
1:4). Paul is writing in an abbreviated fashion here, leaving
out many points that he would include in his argument if the
verse were intended as a completely reasoned statement of the

truth. We remember from high-school algebra that for one familiar with solving equations it was not always necessary to work out every individual step to get the answer. For instance, if one has the equation $2a-10=10$, it is possible to work out the answer laboriously like this: $2a-10=10$; $2a=10+10$; $2a=20$; $a=10$. But only a beginner in algebra does that. A student familiar with the terms can see at a glance that if $2a-10=10$, then $a=10$. It is not necessary to work out the intermediate steps.

That is similar to what Paul does in the opening verses of Romans. He argues that since Jesus has been raised from the dead, Jesus is God. But if he were to spell out his logic, in detail, it would go like this.

(1) Jesus claimed to be God's Son in a special sense. He argued that God was his Father (Jn. 5:18). He said that he had come into this world from the Father and that when he left the world he would return to him (Jn. 16:28). He claimed that whoever had seen him had seen the Father (Jn. 14:9). Those statements were all claims to divinity, and because of them the religious leaders killed him.

(2) Those claims are either true or false. Jesus cannot be partly God and partly not. Either he is who he said he is, or he is a liar.

(3) If those claims are false, they are deceitful and blasphemous.

(4) If they are blasphemous, it is inconceivable that God could honor the one who made them.

(5) But God did honor Jesus by raising him from the dead. God vindicated his claims.

(6) Hence, Jesus is the unique Son of God.

Such an analysis is not just reading into Romans 1:4 what we want to find there. The Bible uses that proof at other points, and Paul is merely echoing that teaching. Jesus used the proof when he appealed to the "sign of the prophet Jonah." He had demonstrated unique authority in his teaching and miracles, but many who heard disbelieved. The rulers asked for a sign. Jesus replied that the only sign given would be that of the prophet Jonah, for "as Jonah was three days and three nights in the belly of the whale, so will the Son of man be three days and three nights in the heart of the earth" (Mt. 12: 40). After that there would be a resurrection, and Christ's unique authority would be vindicated. Similarly, at Pentecost and in the other sermons recorded in Acts, the early disciples used the resurrection to prove Christ's divinity.

Two Guides, Two Tourists

Third, the resurrection of Jesus establishes the doctrine that all who believe in Christ are justified from all sin. Paul also teaches that in Romans. "Jesus . . . was put to death for our trespasses and raised for our justification" (4:24-25). It might better be translated, "Jesus was put to death because we had transgressed, and he was raised because we were justified." The resurrection is God's declaration that he has accepted the sacrifice of Jesus Christ for human sin.

When Jesus was on earth he claimed that he would atone for our sin. "The Son of man came not to be served but to serve, and to give his life as a ransom for many" (Mt. 20:28). In time the hour of his crucifixion came and Jesus died. The sacrifice was offered, the atonement made. But how were human beings to know that it was acceptable? Suppose that Jesus himself had sinned, even while hanging on the cross. In that case the Lamb would not have been without spot or blemish, and the atonement would not have been perfect. Will God accept the sacrifice? For three days the question remains unanswered. Then the moment of the resurrection comes. The hand of God reaches down into the cold Judean tomb, and the body of Christ is quickened. He rises. The stone is rolled away. Jesus is exalted to the right hand of the Father. By these acts we know that God has accepted the perfect sacrifice of his Son for sin.

When Jesus died, He died as my representative, and I died in Him; when He arose, He rose as my representative, and I arose in Him; when He ascended up on high and took His place at the right hand of the Father in the glory, He ascended as my representative and I ascended in Him, and today I am seated in Christ with God in the heavenlies. I look at the cross of Christ, and I know that atonement has been made for my sins; I look at the open sepulcher and the risen and ascended Lord, and I know the atonement has been accepted. There no longer remains a single sin on me, no matter how many or how great my sins may have been.[3]

Fourth, the resurrection of Jesus is also proof that the Christian can live a life that is pleasing to God. The Bible's teaching that by God's standards there is no good in people is true of Christians as much as of unbelievers. Human beings can do good things if we measure them by human standards. There have been outstanding humanitarians and philanthropists among unbelievers. But no one can do good when measured by God's standard, for all that we do is corrupted by our touch. There can be no human victory over sin. But if Jesus is living, then his life can be lived out in us and genuine holiness is possible. This happens by "the immeasurable greatness of his power in us who believe, according to the working of his great might which he accomplished in Christ when he raised him from the dead" (Eph. 1:19-20).

Paul also writes, "We were buried therefore with him by baptism into death, so that as Christ was raised from the dead by the glory of the Father, we too might walk in newness of life" (Rom. 6:4). This means that all who believe in Christ are united to him so that his life becomes available to them. We may be weak and utterly helpless, unable to resist temptation for a single minute. But he is strong, and he lives to give help and deliverance at every moment. Victory, therefore, is no longer a question of my strength but of his power. His power is what we need.

Torrey tells a story that illustrates the point. Four men were once climbing the most difficult face of the Matterhorn. A guide, a tourist, a second guide and a second tourist were all roped together. As they went over a particularly difficult place, the lower tourist lost his footing and went over the side. The sudden pull on the rope carried the lower guide with him, and he carried the other tourist along also. Three men were now dangling over the dizzying cliff. But the guide who was in the lead, feeling the first pull upon the rope, drove his ax into the ice, braced his feet and held fast. The first tourist then regained his footing, the guide regained his, and the lower tourist followed. They then went on and up in safety.

So it is in this life. As the human race ascended the icy cliffs of life, the first Adam lost his footing and tumbled headlong over the abyss. He pulled the next person after him, and the next and the next until the whole race hung in deadly peril. But the last Adam, the Lord Jesus Christ, kept his footing. He stood fast. Thus, all who are united to him by a living faith are secure and can regain the path.

Where Is Thy Sting?

Fifth, the resurrection of Jesus is proof that death is not the end of this life. Death is, in fact, defeated for all who by faith are united to him. When Jesus was here on earth he said to his disciples, "When I go and prepare a place for you, I will come again and will take you to myself, that where I am you may be also" (Jn. 14:3). These verses presuppose the disciples' own resurrection. Similarly, the apostle Paul writes, "For since we believe that Jesus died and rose again, even so, through Jesus, God will bring with him those who have fallen asleep" (1 Thess. 4:14). The believer in Christ is united to Christ by faith in such a manner that if Jesus rose from the dead, the believer must be raised also. We were united to him in death. So also will we be in the resurrection.

At this point two truths must stand out. First, apart from the resurrection of Jesus Christ there is no certainty of life beyond the grave for anyone. And second, on the basis of the resurrection of Jesus Christ, the believer can have perfect confidence. The writings of philosophers have many arguments for immortality, but at best they offer only speculation that such things may be. One philosopher has called the doctrine of immortality "a candle flickering at the end of a dark tunnel." Another has called it "a star shining dimly on the blackest of nights." That is the philosophical hope of immortality, but it does not give confidence. It is a probability but not a certainty. The only sure evidence of our resurrection is the resurrection of Jesus himself, who said, "Because I live, you will live also" (Jn. 14:19). His resurrection makes all the difference.

In the year 1899 two famous men died in America. One was an unbeliever who had made a career of debunking the Bible and arguing against Christian doctrines. The other was a Christian. Colonel Robert G. Ingersoll, after whom the famous Ingersoll lectures on immortality at Harvard University are named, was the unbeliever. He died suddenly, his death coming as an unmitigated shock to his family. The body was kept in the home for several days because Ingersoll's wife could not bear to part with it; it was finally removed because the corpse was decaying and the health of the family required it. At length the remains were cremated, and the display at the crematorium was so dismal that some of the scene was even picked up by the newspapers and communicated to the nation at large. Ingersoll had used his great intellect to deny the resurrection, but when death came there was no hope. His departure was received by his relatives and friends as an uncompensated tragedy.

In the same year the great evangelist Dwight L. Moody died, but his death was triumphant both for himself and for his family. Moody had been declining for some time, and the family had taken turns being with him. On the morning of his death, his son, who was standing by the bedside, heard him exclaim, "Earth is receding; heaven is opening; God is calling."

"You are dreaming, Father," the son said.

Moody answered, "No, Will, this is no dream. I have been within the gates. I have seen the children's faces." For awhile it seemed as if Moody were reviving, but he began to slip away again. He said, "Is this death? This is not bad; there is no valley. This is bliss. This is glorious." By this time his daughter was present, and she began to pray for his recovery. He said, "No, no, Emma, don't pray for that. God is calling. This is my coronation day. I have been looking forward to it." Shortly after that Moody was received into heaven. At the funeral the family and friends joined in a joyful service. They spoke. They sang hymns. They heard the words proclaimed: "O death, where is thy sting? O grave, where is thy victory? The sting of death is sin; and the strength of sin is the law. But thanks be to God, who giveth us the victory through our Lord Jesus Christ" (1 Cor. 15:55-57 KJV).[4] Moody's death was a part of that victory.

I do not mean to imply that the death of every Christian is equally glorious. Not all feel the force of these doctrines in the moment of their homegoing. But many do. Death can be victorious for a Christian. There is no hope apart from our Lord's resurrection.

Finally, the resurrection of Jesus Christ is also the pledge of a final judgment upon all who reject the gospel. On Mars Hill Paul proclaimed that God "has fixed a day on which he will judge the world in righteousness by a man whom he has appointed, and of this he has given assurance to all men by raising him from the dead" (Acts 17:31). Christ spoke of a final judgment when he was on earth, claiming that he would be the judge. The fact that God raised him from the dead is proof of his claims. It is a pledge that the judgment day is coming.

Men and women imagine that death is the end of all things, particularly when it strikes their enemies. A mosquito bites us; we are annoyed; we swat it and congratulate ourselves that we have seen the end of that mosquito. A fox breaks into the chicken coop and we shoot it. So much for the fox. We have an enemy, but when he is dead we dismiss him from our minds.

So it was with Christ. Jesus came into the world doing good and people resented his holiness. They resented it so much that they tried to find something of which to accuse him. He claimed to be God's Son; they called it blasphemy. He spoke of their sin and of a coming day in which he would judge all humankind; they hated him for it. Eventually they killed him. We can imagine the jubilation in Jerusalem on the high feast day following the crucifixion. Those who had disposed of Christ congratulated themselves. At last they were done with him. They were secure; they would never need to endure his arrogance again. Then came the resurrection, and by that act God declared that death would never be the end of Christ. It could never be the end for him, for he is himself the life. Evil is in the world, but nothing opposed to God will finally conquer. Sin triumphed at the cross, but God triumphed at the resurrection. Christ "appeared once for all at the end of the age to put away sin by the sacrifice of himself . . . and after that comes judgment" (Heb. 9:26-27).

17 VERIFYING THE RESURRECTION

If the resurrection of Jesus Christ demonstrates the points covered in the preceding chapter, it is obviously the best news the world has ever heard. But we ask, "Can any news that good be believed?" That question leads to an investigation of the evidences for the resurrection.

Some modern theologians maintain that we have no need for historical evidences for the resurrection of Jesus Christ or evidences of any other point of Christian belief for that matter. Such things are supposed to be authenticated by the logic of faith alone. There is, of course, a sense in which that is true. Christians know that their faith rests not on their ability to demonstrate the truthfulness of the biblical narratives but rather on supernatural activity of the Holy Spirit within their hearts leading them to faith. Yet many come to faith through the various evidences for the resurrection, and the substance and form of the Christian faith rests upon those evidences. Apart from them our experiences of Christ could be mystical and even quite wrong.

We have every right to investigate the evidences, for the Bible itself speaks of "many infallible proofs" of the resurrection (Acts 1:3 KJV). We want to look at six of them in this chapter.

The Ring of Truth

A first important evidence for the resurrection of Jesus Christ is that of the resurrection narratives themselves. There are four of them, one in each Gospel, and more or less independent. Yet they are also harmonious, and that suggests their reliability as historical documents.

That the accounts are basically independent is evident from the considerable variations of detail. Of course there might be some overlap simply because a given incident was circulating throughout the Christian church when these books were being written. An account could have been told by different people at times in nearly identical language. But the four writers obviously did not sit down together and conspire to make up the story of Christ's resurrection. If four people had sat down together and said, "Let's invent an account of a resurrection of Jesus Christ" and had then worked out the details of their stories, there would be far more agreement than we find. We would not find the many small apparent contradictions. Yet if the story were not true and they had somehow separately made it up, it is impossible that we should have the essential agreement we find. In other words, the nature of the narratives is what we would expect from four separate accounts prepared by eyewitnesses.

Here are two examples. First, there is the variety of statements about the moment at which the women first arrived at the tomb. Matthew says that it was "toward the dawn of the first day of the week" (Mt. 28:1). Mark says that it was "very early on the first day of the week . . . when the sun had risen" (Mk. 16:2). Luke says that it was "at early dawn" (Lk. 24:1). John says that "it was still dark" (Jn. 20:1). These phrases are the kind of thing the authors would have standardized if they had been working on their accounts together. But they are in no real contradiction. For one thing, although John says that it was "still dark," he obviously does not mean that it was pitch black; the next phrase says that Mary Magdalene "saw that the stone had been taken away from the tomb." The women may have started out while it was yet dark but arrived at the garden as day was breaking.

A second example of variation in detail in the midst of essential harmony is the listing of the women who made the first visit to the garden. Matthew says there were two Marys, "Mary Magdalene and the other Mary" (Mt. 28:1). Mark writes, "Mary Magdalene, and Mary the mother of James, and Salome" (Mk. 16:1). Luke refers to "Mary Magdalene and Jo-anna and Mary the mother of James and the other women with them" (Lk. 24:10). John mentions only "Mary Magdalene" (Jn. 20:1). Actually, one reference throws light on the others. Mark and Luke, for example, explain who Matthew's "other Mary" was. When we put them together we find that on that first Easter morning, when it was still dark, at least five women set out for the tomb: Mary Magdalene (who is mentioned by each of the writers), Mary the mother of James, Salome, Jo-anna, and at least one other unnamed woman (who fits into Luke's reference to "other women," which includes Salome). The purpose of their trip is to anoint Christ's body. They already know of the difficulty they face, for the tomb had been sealed by a large stone and they have no idea how they can move it. It begins to lighten a bit as they travel, so when they finally draw close to the tomb they see that the stone has been moved. That is something they were not expecting; so, although it suits their purpose, they are nevertheless upset and uncertain what to do. Apparently, they send Mary Magdalene back to tell Peter and John about the new development, which John himself records, although he does not mention the presence of the other women (Jn. 20:2). As the women wait for her to return, the morning grows lighter; eventually, emboldened by daybreak, the women go forward. Now they see the angels and are sent back into the city by them to tell the other disciples (Mt. 28:5-7; Mk. 16:5-7; Lk. 24:4-7).

In the meantime, Mary Magdalene has found Peter and John, who immediately leave her behind them and run to the tomb. John records their view of the graveclothes and points out that it was at this moment that he personally believed (Jn. 20:3-9). Finally, Mary Magdalene arrives back at the tomb again and is the first to see Jesus (Jn. 20:11-18; cf. Mk. 16:9). On the same day Jesus also appears to the other women as they are returning from the tomb, to Peter, to the Emmaus disciples, and to the others as they are gathered together that evening in Jerusalem.

Two other factors also strongly suggest that these are accurate historical accounts. The first is that they leave problems for the reader that would have been eliminated were they fictitious. For example, there is the problem, repeated several times over, that the disciples did not always recognize Jesus when he appeared to them. Mary did not recognize him in the garden (Jn. 20:14). The Emmaus disciples did not know who he was (Lk. 24:16). Even much later, when he appeared to many of the disciples in Galilee, we are told that "some doubted" (Mt. 28:17). From the point of view of persuasion, the inclusion of such details is foolish. The skeptic who reads them will say, "It is obvious that the reason why the disciples did not immediately recognize Jesus is that he was actually someone else. Only the gullible believed, and that was because they wanted to believe. They were self-deluded." Whatever can be said for that argument, the point is that the reason why such problems were allowed to remain in the narrative is that they are, in fact, the way the appearances happened. Consequently, they at least provide strong evidence that these are honest reports of what the writers believed to have transpired.

Another example of a problem is Christ's statement to Mary

that she was not to touch him because he was "not yet ascended to the Father" (Jn. 20:17). Yet Matthew tells us that,
when Jesus appeared to the other women, presumably within
minutes of his appearance to Mary, they "took hold of his feet
and worshiped him" (Mt. 28:9). In the whole history of the
Christian church no one has given a thoroughly convincing
explanation of that anomaly. But it is allowed to stand because, whatever the reason, that is what happened.

Finally, the accounts evidence a fundamental honesty and
accuracy through what we can only call their natural simplicity. If we were setting out to write an account of Christ's resurrection and resurrection appearances, could we have resisted
the urge to describe the resurrection itself—the descent of the
angel, the moving of the stone, the appearance of the Lord
from within the recesses of the tomb? Could we have resisted
the urge to recount how he appeared to Pilate and confounded him? Or how he appeared to Caiaphas and the other
members of the Jewish Sanhedrin? The various apocryphal
Gospels (the Gospel according to the Hebrews, the Gospel of
Peter, the Acts of Pilate and others) contain these elements.
Yet the Gospel writers include none, because either they did
not happen or else the writers themselves did not witness
them. The Gospels do not describe the resurrection because
no one actually witnessed it. It would have made good copy,
but the disciples all arrived at the tomb after Jesus had been
raised.

A second major evidence for the resurrection of Jesus
Christ is the empty tomb. We might deny that an actual resurrection took place, but we can hardly deny that the tomb was
empty. The disciples began soon after the crucifixion and
burial to preach about the resurrection, at a time when those
to whom they preached could simply walk to the tomb to see if
the body of the supposedly resurrected Lord still lay there.

The empty tomb has been so formidable an argument for
the resurrection throughout history that unbelievers have in-

vented a number of theories to account for it. One theory is that the women and later the disciples went to the wrong place. It is conceivable that in the dark the women might have made such an error. But, as we have seen, it was not entirely dark, and besides they had been there earlier and thus were acquainted with its location. Again, we cannot suppose that John and Peter and then all the others would make an identical error.

Another theory is the so-called swoon theory. According to that view, Jesus did not die on the cross but rather swooned—as a result of which he was taken for dead and then buried alive. In the cool of the tomb he revived, moved the stone, and went forth to appear as resurrected. But that explanation has numerous problems. There are the difficulties in believing that a Roman guard entrusted with an execution could be fooled in such a manner; or that the spear thrust into Christ's side would not have killed him even if he had been swooning; or that a weak, barely surviving Christ could have had the strength to move the large stone and overcome Roman guards. Further, one would have to suppose that a Christ in such a condition could convince his disciples that he had overcome death triumphantly.

Finally, there are the views that someone either stole or simply moved the body. But who? Certainly not the disciples, for if they had removed the body, they would later hardly have been willing to die for what they knew to be a fabrication. Nor would the Jewish or Roman authorities have taken the body. We might imagine that they could have moved it initially in order better to guard it—for the same reasons they sealed the tomb and posted a watch: "We remember how that imposter said, while he was still alive, 'After three days I will rise again.' Therefore order the sepulchre to be made secure until the third day, lest his disciples go and steal him away, and tell the people, 'He has risen from the dead' " (Mt. 27:63-64). If that had happened, they would certainly have produced the body later when the disciples began their preaching. The authorities hated the gospel and did everything in their power to stop its spread. They arrested the apostles, threatened them and eventually killed some of them. None of that would have been necessary if they could have produced the body. The obvious reason why they did not is that they could not. The tomb was empty. The body was gone.[1]

A Not Quite Empty Tomb

According to John, the tomb was not quite empty. The body of Jesus was gone but the graveclothes remained behind. The narrative suggests that there was something about them so striking that at least John saw them and believed in Jesus' resurrection.

Every society has its distinct modes of burial, and that was true in ancient cultures as today. In Egypt bodies were embalmed. In Italy and Greece they were often cremated. In Palestine they were wrapped in linen bands that enclosed dry spices and were placed face up without a coffin in tombs generally cut from the rock in the Judean and Galilean hills. Many such tombs still exist and can be seen by any visitor to Palestine.

Another aspect of Jewish burial in ancient times is of special interest for understanding John's account of Jesus' resurrection. In a book called *The Risen Master* (1901), Henry Latham calls attention to a unique feature of Eastern burials, which he noticed when in Constantinople during the last century. He says that the funerals he witnessed there varied in many respects, depending upon whether the funeral was for a poor or rich person. But in one respect all the arrangements were identical. Latham noticed that the bodies were wrapped in linen cloths in such a manner as to leave the face, neck and upper part of the shoulders bare. The upper part of the head was covered by a cloth that had been twirled about it like a turban. Latham concluded that since burial styles change slowly, particularly in the East, that mode of burial may well have been practiced in Jesus' time.

Luke tells us that when Jesus was approaching the village of Nain earlier in his ministry, he met a funeral procession leaving the city. The only son of a widow had died. Luke says that when Jesus raised him from death two things happened. First, the young man sat up, that is, he was lying on his back on the bier without a coffin. And second, he at once began to speak. Hence, the graveclothes did not cover his face. Separate coverings for the head and body were also used in the burial of Lazarus (Jn. 11:44).

It must have been in a similar manner that Joseph of Arimathea and Nicodemus buried Jesus Christ. The body of Jesus was removed from the cross before the beginning of the Jewish sabbath, was washed, and then was wrapped in linen bands. One hundred pounds of dry spices were carefully inserted into the folds of the linen. One of them, aloes, was a powdered wood like fine sawdust with an aromatic fragrance; another, myrrh, was a fragrant gum that would be carefully mixed with the powder. Jesus' body was thus encased. His head, neck and upper shoulders were left bare. A linen cloth was wrapped about the upper part of his head like a turban. The body was then placed within the tomb where it lay until sometime on Saturday night or Sunday morning.

What would we have seen had we been there at the moment at which Jesus was raised from the dead? Would we have seen him stir, open his eyes, sit up, and begin to struggle out of the bandages? We must remember that it would have been difficult to escape from the bandages. Is that what we would have seen? Not at all. That would have been a resuscitation, not a resurrection. It would have been the same as if he had recovered from a swoon. Jesus would have been raised in a natural body rather than a spiritual body, and that was not what happened.

If we had been present in the tomb at the moment of the

resurrection, we would have noticed that all at once the body of Jesus seemed to disappear. John Stott says that the body was " 'vaporized,' being transmuted into something new and different and wonderful."[2] Latham says that the body had been "exhaled," passing "into a phase of being like that of Moses and Elias on the Mount."[3] We would have seen only that it was gone.

What would have happened then? The linen cloths would have collapsed once the body was removed, because of the weight of the spices, and would have been lying undisturbed where the body of Jesus had been. The cloth which surrounded the head, without the weight of spices, might well have retained its concave shape and have lain by itself separated from the other cloths by the space where the neck and shoulders of the Lord had been.

That is exactly what John and Peter saw when they entered the sepulcher, and the eyewitness account reveals it perfectly. John was the first at the tomb, and as he reached the open sepulcher in the murky light of early dawn he saw the graveclothes lying there. Something about them attracted his attention. First, it was significant that they were lying there at all. John places the word for "lying" at an emphatic position in the Greek sentence. We might translate it, "He saw, lying there, the graveclothes" (Jn. 20:5). Further, the cloths were undisturbed. The word that John uses (*keimena*) is used in the Greek papyri of things that have been carefully placed in order. (One document speaks of legal papers saying, "I have not yet obtained the documents, but they are lying collated." Another speaks of clothes that are "lying [in order] until you send me word.") Certainly John noticed that there had been no disturbance at the tomb.

At that point Peter arrived and went into the sepulcher. Undoubtedly Peter saw what John saw, but in addition he was struck by something else. The cloth that had been around the head was not with the other cloths. It was lying in a place

by itself (Jn. 20:7). And what was more striking, it had retained a circular shape. John says that it was "wrapped together" (KJV). We might say that it was "twirled about itself."
And there was a space between it and the cloths that had envel-
oped the body. The narrative says, "Then Simon Peter came,
following him, and went into the tomb; he saw the linen cloths
lying, and the napkin, which had been on his head, not lying
with the linen cloths but rolled up in a place by itself" (20:6-7).
Finally John too entered the sepulcher and saw what Peter
saw. When he saw it he believed.

What did John believe? He might have explained it to Peter
like this. "Don't you see, Peter, that no one has moved the
body or disturbed the graveclothes? They are lying exactly as
Nicodemus and Joseph of Arimathea left them on the eve of
the sabbath. Yet the body is gone. It has not been stolen. It has
not been moved. Clearly it must have passed through the
clothes, leaving them as we see them now. Jesus must be
risen." Stott says, "A glance at these graveclothes proved the
reality, and indicated the nature, of the resurrection."[4]

Cleopas and Mary Kept Packing

A fourth evidence for the resurrection is the obvious fact that
Jesus was seen by the disciples. According to the various accounts he appeared to Mary Magdalene first of all, then to the
other women who were returning from the tomb, afterward
to Peter, to the Emmaus disciples, to the ten gathered in the
Upper Room, then (a week later) to the eleven disciples including Thomas, to James, to five hundred brethren at once
(1 Cor. 15:6, perhaps on a mountainside in Galilee), to a band
of disciples who had been fishing on the lake of Galilee, to
those who witnessed the ascension from the Mount of Olives
near Jerusalem, and last of all to Paul, who claimed to have
seen Christ in his vision on the road to Damascus. During
the days following the resurrection, all these persons moved
from blank, enervating despair to firm conviction and joy.

Nothing accounts for that but the fact that they had indeed seen Jesus.

During the last century a well-known critic of the Gospels, Ernest Renan, wrote that belief in Christ's resurrection arose from the passion of a hallucinating woman, meaning that Mary Magdalene was in love with Jesus and deluded herself into thinking that she had seen him alive when she had actually only seen the gardener. That is preposterous. The last person in the world that Mary (or any of the others) expected to see was Jesus. The only reason she was in the garden was to anoint his body. Moreover, even if Mary had believed in some sort of resurrection through the power of love, there is no evidence that the disciples could have been so deluded or that they anticipated anything of the kind. Many despaired; some, like the Emmaus disciples, were scattering. Thomas, for one, was adamant in his disbelief. Yet we find that within a matter of days after the Lord's alleged resurrection, all of them were convinced of what beforehand they would have judged impossible. And they went forth to tell about it, persisting in their conviction even in the face of threats, persecution and death.

One clear example of unbelieving disciples being convinced of the resurrection solely by the appearance of Jesus is that of the Emmaus disciples. One of them is identified. He is Cleopas (Lk. 24:18). If he is to be identified with the Clopas (slight variation in spelling) mentioned in John 19:25, then we know that his wife's name was Mary, that she was in Jerusalem, had witnessed the crucifixion along with the other women and was therefore probably the one returning to Emmaus with him on the first Easter morning.

The importance of this identification lies in the fact that Mary, and perhaps Cleopas too, had witnessed the crucifixion and therefore had not the slightest doubt that Jesus was dead. Mary had seen the nails driven into Christ's hands. She had seen the cross erected. She saw the blood. Finally, she saw the spear driven into his side. Afterwards Mary undoubtedly went back to where she was staying. The Passover came, and Mary and Cleopas observed it like good Jews. They waited in sadness over the holidays—from the day of the crucifixion until the day of the resurrection—for the same sabbath restraints on travel that had kept the women from going to the sepulcher to anoint the body would also have kept Cleopas and Mary from returning home to Emmaus. The morning after the Saturday sabbath finally came. It is possible that Mary is one who went to the tomb to anoint the body. If that is the case, she saw the angels, returned to tell Cleopas about it, and then—look how remarkable this is—joined him in preparing to leave. So far from their thinking was any idea of the literal truth of Christ's bodily resurrection!

What is more, during the time that Cleopas and Mary were getting ready to leave, Peter and John set out for the sepulcher. They entered the tomb. Right then John believed in some sense, although he may not have understood all that the resurrection meant. Peter and John returned, told Cleopas, Mary and the others what they had seen. And then—again this is most remarkable—Cleopas and Mary went right on packing. As soon as they were ready, they left Jerusalem. Did that Palestinian peasant couple believe in Christ's resurrection? Certainly not. Did they come to believe, as they eventually did, because of their own or someone else's wishful thinking or a hallucination? No. They were so sad at the loss of Jesus, so miserable, so preoccupied with the reality of his death, that they would not even take twenty or thirty minutes personally to investigate the reports of his resurrection.

If someone should say, "But surely they must not have heard the reports; you are making that part of the story up," the objection is answered by the words of Cleopas. When Jesus appeared to them on the road and asked why they were so sad, Cleopas answered by telling him first about the crucifixion and then adding, "Moreover, some women of our company amazed us. They were at the tomb early in the morning and did not find his body; and they came back saying that they had even seen a vision of angels, who said that he was alive. Some of those who were with us [Peter and John] went to the tomb, and found it just as the women had said; but him they did not see" (Lk. 24:22-24).

What accounts for a belief in the resurrection on the part of Christ's disciples? Nothing but the resurrection itself. If we cannot account for the belief of the disciples in that way, we are faced with the greatest enigma in history. If we account for it by a real resurrection and real appearances of the risen Lord, then Christianity is understandable and offers a sure hope to all.

Transformation of the Disciples

A fifth evidence for the resurrection flows from what has just been said: the transformed character of the disciples.

Take Peter as an example. Before the resurrection Peter is in Jerusalem tagging along quietly behind the arresting party. That night he denies Jesus three times. Later he is in Jerusalem, fearful, shut up behind closed doors along with the other disciples. Yet all is changed following the resurrection. Then Peter is preaching boldly. He says in his first sermon on the day of Pentecost, "Men of Israel, hear these words: Jesus of Nazareth, a man attested to you by God with mighty works and wonders and signs which God did through him in your midst, as you yourselves know—this Jesus, delivered up according to the definite plan and foreknowledge of God, you crucified and killed by the hands of lawless men. But God raised him up, having loosed the pangs of death, because it was not possible for him to be held by it" (Acts 2:22-24). A few chapters farther on in Acts we find him before the Jewish Sanhedrin (the body that condemned Jesus to death), saying, "Whether it is right in the sight of God to listen to you rather than to God, you must judge; for we cannot but speak of what we have seen and heard" (Acts 4:19-20).

"Something tremendous must have happened to account for such a radical and astounding moral transformation as this. Nothing short of the fact of the resurrection, of their having seen the risen Lord, will explain it."[5]

Another example is James, Jesus' brother. At one point none of Jesus' brothers believed in him (Jn. 7:5). Jesus once declared, "A prophet is not without honor except in his own country and in his own house" (Mt. 13:57). But later James does believe (cf. Acts 1:14). What made the difference? Obviously, only the appearance of Jesus to him, which is recorded in 1 Corinthians 15:7.

The final though often overlooked evidence for the resurrection of Jesus Christ is the change of the day of regular Christian worship from the Jewish sabbath (Saturday) to Sunday, the first day of the week. Could anything be more fixed in religious tradition than the setting aside of the seventh day for worship as practiced in Judaism? Hardly. The sanctification of the seventh day was embodied in the law of Moses and had been practiced for centuries. Yet from the very beginning we see Christians, though Jews, disregarding the sabbath as their day of worship and instead worshiping on Sunday. What can account for that? There is no prophecy to that effect, no declaration of an early church council. The only adequate cause is the resurrection of Jesus Christ, an event so significant that it immediately produced the most profound changes, not only in the moral character of the early believers, but in their habits of life and forms of worship as well.

I was once speaking to another minister about his spiritual experience when the conversation turned to the resurrection. The minister said that when he came out of seminary he possessed no real convictions concerning the gospel of Christ. He probably believed some things intellectually, but they had not gripped his heart. He said that he began to reflect on the resurrection. I asked, "What did you find?" First of all, he replied, he discovered a strange happiness and internal rest as he struggled with the accounts and the questions that they forced to his mind. That indicated to him that, although he did not have the answers yet, at least he was on the right track. As he studied he came to see the importance of the issue. He saw that if Jesus really rose from the dead, everything else recorded about him in the New Testament is true—at least there is no sound reason for rejecting it. And he concluded that if Jesus was not raised from the dead, he should leave the ministry.

So he read books. He visited the seminary where he had studied. He talked with his professors. He said that he became convinced that Jesus is indeed risen, as the Bible declares, and that all the other doctrines of the faith stand with it. Interestingly enough, he came to that conclusion several weeks before Easter that particular year, and on Easter he therefore stood up in church to proclaim his personal faith in these things. Afterward members of his congregation said that they had never heard preaching like that before, and several believed in Christ as a result of his preaching.

That has happened to many: to jurists like Frank Morison, Gilbert West, Edward Clark and J. N. D. Anderson; to scholars like James Orr, Michael Ramsey, Arnold H. M. Lunn, Wolfhart Pannenburg and Michael Green. Green says that "the evidence in favor of this astonishing fact is overwhelming."[6] Ramsey wrote, "So utterly new and foreign to the expectations of men was this doctrine, that it seems hard to doubt that only historical events could have created it."[7]

Did Jesus rise from the dead? If he did, then he is the Son of God and our Savior. It is for us to believe and follow him.

18

HE
ASCENDED INTO
HEAVEN

It is always difficult to measure one's own spiritual maturity. But there is a sense in which one can assess it generally by the dominant image one has of Jesus Christ. For example, some persons think of Jesus largely in his Incarnation with the result that their mental picture is basically that of a baby lying in a manger. That is not wrong, of course. The Lord did become a baby in his Incarnation, and the Incarnation itself is an important concept. But it is at best an introductory image of Christ. A more mature image is that of Christ on the cross, which is what other people think of. That is better, because the cross explains the Incarnation. Jesus came to earth to die. "The Son of man came not to be served but to serve, and to give his life as a ransom for many" (Mt. 20:28). Still, good as that image is, it is not good enough. Jesus is no longer dead. An image of the resurrected Christ is necessary to round out the picture. It is the resurrected Christ, not Christ on the cross, who speaks peace to his disciples and commissions them to the task of world evangelization.

The Bible, having spoken of the resurrection, goes on to Christ's ascension to heaven—where he is now seated at the right hand of the Father, ruling his church and awaiting the day in which he shall come forth in power to judge the living and the dead.

The New Testament refers to Christ's ascension in many places. In the Gospel of John it is twice referred to in an anticipatory manner. Jesus asked those disciples who were offended by him, "What if you were to see the Son of man ascending where he was before?" (Jn. 6:62). To Mary Magdalene he said, "Do not hold me, for I have not yet ascended to the Father; but go to my brethren and say to them, I am ascending to my Father and your Father, to my God and your God" (Jn. 20:17). In Acts his ascension is recounted with circumstantial details: "And when he had said this, as they were looking on, he was lifted up, and a cloud took him out of their sight" (Acts 1:9). The same account is found in the longer ending of Mark (16:19) and in Luke 24:51. Later, in the Epistles, the ascension is referred to in speaking of the fullness of Christ's work. "Who is to condemn? Is it Christ Jesus, who died, yes, who was raised from the dead, who is at the right hand of God, who indeed intercedes for us?" (Rom. 8:34). "If then you have been raised with Christ, seek the things that are above, where Christ is, seated at the right hand of God" (Col. 3:1). The letter to the Hebrews makes repeated references to Christ's ascension and present position in heaven (Heb. 1:3; 6:20; 8:1; 9:12, 24; 10:12; 12:2; 13:20). In 1 Timothy the ascension is placed within the full perspective of Christ's work: "Great indeed, we confess, is the mystery of our religion: He was manifested in the flesh, vindicated in the Spirit, seen by angels, preached among the nations, believed on in the world, taken up in glory" (1 Tim. 3:16).

That the ascension of Christ is mentioned so often in the New Testament is a clear indication of its importance. But that does not tell us why it is important or how it relates to us. The verses themselves do give us an explanation of the meaning of the ascension, in three main areas. These are framed succinctly in the well-known words of the Apostles' Creed: "He ascended into heaven, and sitteth on the right hand of God the Father Almighty; from thence he shall come to judge the quick and the dead."

Preparing a Place

The first thing suggested by the ascension of Jesus to heaven is the idea that heaven is a real place. To say that it is a real place does not mean that we can therefore describe it adequately, even with the help of various biblical symbols. The book of Revelation, for example, speaks of it as a city whose streets are paved with gold, whose foundations are massive, where the light never ceases to shine. But heaven is not necessarily an actual city; such language is symbolic. A city speaks of a place to belong, a home. Foundations convey the idea of permanence. Gold suggests that which is precious. Light speaks of the eternal presence and unhindered enjoyment of God by his people.

Yet in recognizing the symbolism we do not want to make the error of supposing that heaven is therefore anything less than a real place, perhaps even as localized as New York or London, for example. The explicit teachings of Christ as well as the ascension itself are meant to teach such a reality.

Some have observed that because God is described as being pure spirit—that is, as having no bodily form—heaven should therefore be described as the state of being spirit. But the idea that heaven is a state and therefore everywhere and nowhere is not what the Bible suggests. We recognize the limitations of talking about something entirely beyond our present experience. But at the same time we notice that although God the Father does not have a concrete, visible form, the second person of the Trinity does. Jesus became man and remains the God-man for eternity. We also will have bodies in the resurrection. Our bodies will be different from what we know now. They will be like Christ's resurrection body, which could move through closed doors, for example. Still they will be real bodies, whatever their mysterious characteristics, and as bodies they must be somewhere. Heaven is the place where our bodies will be. Of course, we will presumably be able to move freely about the universe.

Second, the ascension of Christ speaks to us of his present work, as he himself taught. One aspect of that work is the *sending of the Holy Spirit,* which we should understand not merely as a past sending of the Holy Spirit at Pentecost but also as a present continuous sending of the Holy Spirit to do his work in this world. Jesus said, "It is to your advantage that I go away, for if I do not go away, the Counselor will not come to you; but if I go, I will send him to you" (Jn. 16:7). A second aspect is his intercession on behalf of his people. The book of Hebrews makes much of this, pointing out that Jesus exercises an intercessory role for us as our heavenly high priest.

Third, in speaking of Christ's present work in heaven, we recall his promise to the disciples that he was going to *prepare a place* for them (Jn. 14:2-3). We cannot really know what Jesus is doing in this regard, since we cannot adequately visualize heaven. Nevertheless, we know that in some way he is preparing heaven for us. That assures us of the Lord's present interest in us and of his activity on our behalf.

Position of Honor

The words of the Creed tell us not only that Jesus "ascended into heaven." They also tell us that having ascended into heaven he now "sitteth on the right hand of God the Father Almighty." That image is drawn from the ancient practice of having a person who was particularly favored by a king seated next to him on the right. It speaks of the honor given to that person and of his role in the king's dominion.

That Jesus has been so *honored* is made clear in many places in Scripture. Hebrews 1:3 is an example: "He reflects the glory of God and bears the very stamp of his nature, upholding the universe by his word of power. When he had made purification for sins, he sat down at the right hand of the Majesty on high." Here, as Charles Hodge points out, "The ground of Christ's exaltation is twofold: the possession of divine attributes by which he was entitled to divine honor and was qualified to exercise absolute and universal dominion; and secondly, his mediatorial work."[1] Again, although specific reference to Christ's being seated at God's right hand is omitted, Philippians 2:5-11 gives a similar basis for Christ being honored. It is because he possessed "equality with God" but nevertheless "emptied himself" and became "obedient unto death" for our salvation. "Therefore God has highly exalted him and bestowed on him the name which is above every name, that at the name of Jesus every knee should bow, in heaven and on earth and under the earth, and every tongue confess that Jesus Christ is Lord, to the glory of God the Father" (2:9-11).

Christ's position at the Father's right hand also speaks of the Lord's present *authority* over the world and the church. It is the authority he spoke of prior to his ascension but following his resurrection. "All authority in heaven and on earth has been given to me. Go therefore and make disciples of all nations, baptizing them in the name of the Father and of the Son and of the Holy Spirit, teaching them to observe all that I have commanded you; and lo, I am with you always, to the close of the age" (Mt. 28:18-20). It is impossible to overestimate the scope of Christ's authority. The announcement is not merely that authority has been given to him but that *all* authority has been given to him. Then, lest we still misunderstand or minimize his authority, he goes on to declare that it is an authority exercised both in heaven and on earth.

That all authority in heaven has been given to Jesus could mean merely that the authority he was to exercise on earth would be recognized in heaven also. If so, it would be a good statement of Christ's full divinity—for that authority is God's authority. Yet there is probably more to Christ's statement than that. For one thing, we remember that when the Bible talks about "powers" or "authorities" in heaven it is usually talking about spiritual or demonic powers. When it talks about Christ's victory through his death and resurrection it usually has those powers in mind as well. "For we are not contending against flesh and blood, but against the principalities, against the powers, against the world rulers of this present darkness, against the spiritual hosts of wickedness in the heavenly places" (Eph. 6:12). Or again, we think of those verses early in the same letter that speak of the greatness of God's power "which he accomplished in Christ when he raised him from the dead and made him sit at his right hand in the heavenly places, far above all rule and authority and power and dominion, and above every name that is named, not only in this age but also in that which is to come" (Eph. 1:20-21).

When we put Christ's announcement into that context we sense that what the Lord is talking about is not so much an acknowledgment of his earthly authority in heaven as a declaration that his authority is over all other authorities whether spiritual, demonic or otherwise. His resurrection demonstrates his authority over any power that can possibly be imagined. Consequently, we do not fear Satan or anyone else while we are engaged in Christ's service.

Second, Jesus announces that he has authority over everything on earth. This has several dimensions. It means that he has authority over us, his people. If we are truly his people, it means that we have come to him confessing that we are sinners, that he is the divine Savior, and that we have accepted his sacrifice on our behalf and have pledged ourselves to follow him as Lord. That is hypocrisy if it does not contain a recognition of his authority over us in every area. To be sure, there are other legitimate though lesser authorities over us as well: the authority of parents over children, of officers within the church, of state authorities. But he is the King of kings and Lord of lords.

The declaration of Christ's authority on earth also means that he has authority over those who are not yet believers. That is, his authority extends to the "nations" to whom he sends us with the gospel (Mt. 28:19). This means, on the one hand, that the religion of our Lord is to be a world religion. No one is outside the sphere of his authority or to be exempt from his call. On the other hand, it is also a statement of his ability to bring fruit from our efforts, for it is through the exercise of his authority that men and women actually come to believe in him and follow him.

The fundamental basis of all Christian missionary enterprise is the universal authority of Jesus Christ, "in heaven and on earth." If the authority of Jesus were circumscribed on earth, if he were but one of many religious teachers, one of many Jewish prophets, one of many divine incarnations, we would have no mandate to present him to the nations as the Lord and Savior of the world. If the authority of Jesus were limited in heaven, if he had not decisively overthrown the principalities and powers, we might still proclaim him to the nations, but we would never be able to "turn them from darkness to light, and from the power of Satan unto God" (Acts 26:18). Only because all authority on earth belongs to Christ dare we go to all nations. And only because all authority in heaven as well is his have we any hope of success.[2]

Vision of Christ

Finally, we have the last picture of which the Apostles' Creed speaks, the picture of Christ coming from heaven "to judge the quick [living] and the dead." There is a reluctance today to talk about judgment, as we pointed out when speaking of God's wrath. Judgment is thought to be ignoble. We can talk about God's love, grace, mercy, care, compassion, strength. We can say he is the answer to whatever problem we have, that he is adequate for every emergency. But to talk about God as a God of judgment and of Jesus Christ as a judge is so offensive to our culture that many let this doctrine pass.

How can we possibly overlook the fact that the great and holy God of the universe will one day judge sin? If it were not true that God will judge sin, it would be a blot on the name of God. We could not talk about a holy God, a just God, a sovereign God, if he were to let sin go on unchecked indefinitely as he obviously seems to let it do for a time in this world. We may object that sometimes sin *is* punished in this world. Sin has its built-in, self-destructing mechanisms. But to be honest we must admit that sometimes good people suffer also, and sometimes evildoers go free. Although the evildoer is sometimes punished, no one would seriously maintain that all evil is properly punished and all good properly rewarded *in this world.* So if there is not a final judgment in which the inequities of this life are made right, there is no righteousness in God. There is no ultimate justice anywhere.

But according to the teaching of the Bible, there is justice and there will be a judgment. Whenever we begin to talk of justice before God, there is a sense in which we should rightly draw back in horror. It is not just a matter of this particular good deed, which we imagine ourselves to have done, being rewarded, and that particular bad deed being judged. It is rather that by God's standards "None is righteous, no, not one; no one understands, no one seeks for God. All have turned aside, together they have gone wrong; no one does good, not even one" (Rom. 3:10-12). To speak of the judgment of God is to speak of judgment that rightly falls upon all of us. What shall we do then? How shall we stand before Christ in that judgment?

There is a beautiful picture in the book of Acts of how the Christian can stand before God. It is a picture of how the one who has believed in Christ will find him—miracle of miracles —not as judge but redeemer. The picture comes to us from the account of the death of Stephen, a common person who had preached in Jerusalem with such power that the authorities hated him and had him stoned to death. Before he died, however, God granted him a vision of the heavenly Christ. He saw Jesus, not seated on the throne of judgment at the right hand of God, but rather standing at God's side to welcome him to glory. His testimony was "Behold, I see the heavens opened, and the Son of man standing at the right hand of God" (Acts 7:56). As he died he repeated his Lord's own statements: "Lord Jesus, receive my spirit" (7:59) and "Lord, do not hold this sin against them" (7:60).

Jesus is the source in which all spiritual good may be found. *If we seek strength, it lies in his dominion; if purity, in his conception; if gentleness, it appears in his birth. For by his birth he was made like us in all respects (Heb. 2:17) that he might learn to feel our pain (cf. Heb. 5:2). If we seek redemption, it lies in his passion; if acquittal, in his condemnation; if remission of the curse, in his cross (Gal. 3:13); if satisfaction, in his sacrifice; if purification, in his blood; if reconciliation, in his descent into hell; if mortification of the flesh, in his tomb; if newness of life, in his resurrection; if immortality, in the same; if inheritance of the Heavenly Kingdom, in his entrance into heaven; if protection, if security, if abundant supply of all blessings, in his Kingdom; if untroubled expectation of judgment, in the power given to him to judge.*[3]
In view of Christ's person and work it is foolish to seek for spiritual blessing elsewhere. It is wise to trust him only.

NOTES

Chapter 1
[1]Reinhold Niebuhr, *The Nature and Destiny of Man*, one-volume edition of the Gifford Lectures on "Human Nature" and "Human Destiny" (New York: Charles Scribner's Sons, 1949), Part 1, p. 1.
[2]Quoted in Niebuhr, pp. 9-10.
[3]Ibid., p. 1.
[4]Ibid., p. 121.
[5]Emil Brunner, *The Christian Doctrine of Creation and Redemption: Dogmatics,* II trans. Olive Wyon (Philadelphia: Westminster, 1952), p. 91.
[6]Ibid.
[7]Ibid.
[8]C. S. Lewis, *Mere Christianity* (New York: Macmillan, 1958), p. 94.

Chapter 2
[1]See *The Sovereign God* (Downers Grove: InterVarsity Press, 1978), pp. 195-99.
[2]John R. W. Stott, *Basic Christianity* (Grand Rapids, Mich.: Eerdmans, 1958), pp. 72, 75.

Chapter 3
[1]Martin Luther, *The Bondage of the Will,* trans. J. I. Packer and O. R. Johnston (Westwood, N.J.: Fleming H. Revell, 1957), p. 319.
[2]Brunner, p. 121.
[3]Brunner, p. 118.
[4]Arthur W. Pink, *The Sovereignty of God* (Grand Rapids, Mich.: Baker, 1969), pp. 187-88.

[5]I have discussed this subject in a similar way but at somewhat greater length in *The Gospel of John,* II (Grand Rapids, Mich.: Zondervan, 1976), pp. 167-69.

Chapter 4

[1]Compare the article on *nomos* ("law") in the *Theological Dictionary of the New Testament,* ed. Gerhard Kittel and trans. Geoffrey W. Bromiley, IV (Grand Rapids, Mich.: Eerdmans, 1967), pp. 1022-85, particularly pp. 1044-46.

[2]John Calvin, *The Institutes of the Christian Religion,* I, ed. John T. McNeill and trans. Ford Lewis Battles (Philadelphia: Westminster, 1960), pp. 358-59.

[3]Ibid., p. 355.

Chapter 5

[1]Stott, p. 65.

[2]J. I. Packer, *Knowing God* (Downers Grove: InterVarsity Press, 1973), p. 40.

[3]Ibid., p. 41. There is a discussion of this same theme in the first volume of these studies (*The Sovereign God,* pp. 133-35).

[4]Calvin, p. 388.

[5]Ibid., p. 399.

Chapter 6

[1]Thomas Watson, *The Ten Commandments* (1692; rpt. London: The Banner of Truth Trust, 1970), p. 122.

[2]Calvin, p. 401.

[3]I have discussed this same theme at somewhat greater length in *The Sermon on the Mount* (Grand Rapids, Mich.: Zondervan, 1972), pp. 105-11.

[4]Lewis, p. 75.

[5]The material on contemporary sexual morality also occurs in my book, *The Sermon on the Mount,* pp. 112-15. A full discussion of Christ's interpretation of the seventh commandment and the divorce question occupies pp. 112-48.

[6]Stott, p. 69.

Chapter 7

[1]Niebuhr, p. 131.

[2]Packer, pp. 134-35.

[3]Leon Morris, *The Apostolic Preaching of the Cross* (Grand Rapids, Mich.: Eerdmans, 1956), pp. 162-63.

[4]The best example here is C. H. Dodd (*The Epistle of Paul to the Romans,* London: Hodder and Stoughton, 1932, p. 20ff., and other writings), but he is only one of many.

Chapter 9

[1]Brunner, p. 339.

[2]J. A. Motyer, *Philippian Studies: The Richness of Christ* (Chicago: InterVarsity Press, 1966), p. 74.

[3]Handley C. G. Moule, *Philippian Studies: Lessons in Faith and Love* (Lon-

don: Pickering and Inglis, n.d.), p. 97.

[4]For a full discussion of these and other texts see Benjamin Breckinridge Warfield, "The Person of Christ According to the New Testament," in *The Person and Work of Christ* (Philadelphia: The Presbyterian and Reformed Publishing Company, 1970), pp. 38-47.

[5]Ibid., p. 47.

[6]Stott, p. 26.

[7]Ibid., p. 32.

[8]Lewis, p. 41.

[9]I have borrowed parts of this last section from my own *The Gospel of John,* II, pp. 252-57.

Chapter 10

[1]Alexander Ross, *The Epistles of James and John,* "New International Commentary on the New Testament" (Grand Rapids, Mich.: Eerdmans, 1954), p. 115.

[2]Warfield, "On the Emotional Life of Our Lord," pp. 93-145.

[3]R. H. Lightfoot, *St. John's Gospel: A Commentary* (Oxford: The University Press, 1963), p. 229.

[4]G. Campbell Morgan, *The Gospel According to John* (Westwood, N.J.: Fleming H. Revell, n.d.), p. 197.

[5]Warfield, pp. 122-23.

Chapter 11

[1]James Denney, *The Death of Christ,* ed. R. V. G. Tasker (Chicago: Inter-Varsity Press, 1964), p. 175.

[2]One of the most important themes of Anselm's work is in this area, in justification of inquiry into the reason for certain revealed truths. His phrase for this is *fides quaerens intellectum* ("faith in search of understanding"). It is the subject of a valuable study by Karl Barth, *Anselm: Fides Quaerens Intellectum* (Richmond: John Knox Press, 1958).

[3]Eugene R. Fairweather, ed. and trans., *A Scholastic Miscellany: Anselm to Ockham,* "The Library of Christian Classics," X (Philadelphia: The Westminster Press, 1956), p. 176.

[4]H. E. Guillebaud, *Why the Cross?* (Chicago: Inter-Varsity Christian Fellowship, 1947), pp. 130, 185.

[5]Packer, p. 51.

Chapter 12

[1]Charles Hodge, *Systematic Theology,* II (London: James Clarke & Co., 1960), p. 461. Martin Luther was probably the first to teach explicitly that Christ was a prophet, priest and king, but he never spoke of this as a "threefold office." That distinction belongs to John Calvin who, with his greater gift for systematization, develops it fully in Book 2 of the *Institutes of the Christian Religion* (ch. 15). From this point it is seen often in Protestant writings, particularly those of the English and American Puritans. The Westminster Confession of Faith mentions the three offices in the chapter "Of Christ the Mediator." The Shorter Catechism asks in

which way Christ "doth... execute" these offices, and replies: "Christ executeth the office of a prophet in revealing to us, by his Word and Spirit, the will of God for our salvation.... Christ executeth the office of a priest in his once offering up of himself a sacrifice to satisfy divine justice and reconcile us to God, and in making continual intercession for us.... Christ executeth the office of a king in subduing us to himself, in ruling and defending us, and in restraining and conquering all his and our enemies" (Q. 24, 25, 26).

[2]Stott, p. 22.

[3]I have discussed the Logos concept at greater length both in *The Gospel of John*, I (Grand Rapids, Mich.: Zondervan, 1975), pp. 37-42, and in *Witness and Revelation in the Gospel of John* (Grand Rapids: Zondervan, 1970), pp. 159-63.

[4]Some material on the kingdom of God has been borrowed from my work, *The Sermon on the Mount*, pp. 205-11.

Chapter 13

[1]Dodd's basic contention is that there is no such thing as wrath in God occasioned by human sin. Therefore, since there is no wrath, the meaning "propitiation" is incorrect in the New Testament, even though the word it translates (*hilasmos, hilastērion*) may well have the idea of propitiation in pagan religion. He believes that the Bible deals only with the putting away of sin and thus that "expiation" is the better rendering.

[2]Packer, p. 165.

[3]Morris, p. 179.

[4]Packer, p. 170. The meaning of propitiation is discussed by Packer in some detail (pp. 161-80). It is also discussed at length by Morris, pp. 125-85; Warfield, pp. 351-426; T. C. Hammond, *In Understanding Be Men* (Downers Grove: InterVarsity Press, 1968), pp. 116-27; Guillebaud; and Denney.

[5]Packer, p. 171.

Chapter 14

[1]Warfield, "Redeemer and Redemption," p. 325. This, the opening address for the year, was delivered in Miller Chapel, September 17, 1915, and appeared first in *The Princeton Theological Review*, XIV, 1916, pp. 177-201.

[2]Morris, p. 22. This and other examples are taken from *Light from the Ancient East* by Adolf Deissman.

[3]This has been discussed at some length in *The Sovereign God*, pp. 206-09, and in the first chapter of the present volume.

Chapter 15

[1]Augustine, *The Gospel According to St. John*, cx, 6 in *The Nicene and Post-Nicene Fathers*, first series, ed. by Philip Schaff (New York: The Christian Literature Company, 1888), Vol. 7, p. 41.

[2]C. S. Lewis, *The Four Loves* (New York: Harcourt, Brace & World, 1960), pp. 175-76.

[3]Ibid., p. 11.

[4]Packer, pp. 112-13.

Chapter 16

[1]See C. H. Dodd, *The Apostolic Preaching and Its Developments* (New York: Harper & Bros., n.d.).

[2]R. A. Torrey, *The Uplifted Christ* (Grand Rapids, Mich.: Zondervan, 1965), pp. 70-71.

[3]R. A. Torrey, *The Bible and Its Christ* (Old Tappan, N.J.: Fleming H. Revell, n.d.), pp. 107-08.

[4]I have told the story of the death of Ingersoll and Moody in *Philippians: An Expositional Commentary* (Grand Rapids, Mich.: Zondervan, 1971), pp. 256-57.

Chapter 17

[1]The evidence of the empty tomb is discussed at greater length by Stott, pp. 46-50; Merrill C. Tenney, *The Reality of the Resurrection* (Chicago: Moody Press, 1963), pp. 113-16; James Orr, *The Resurrection of Jesus* (London: Hodder and Stoughton, n.d.), pp. 111-39; and others.

[2]Stott, p. 52.

[3]Henry Latham, *The Risen Master* (Cambridge: Deighton Bell and Company, 1901), pp. 36, 54.

[4]Stott, p. 53.

[5]Torrey, *The Bible and Its Christ*, p. 92.

[6]Michael Green, *Runaway World* (Downers Grove: InterVarsity Press, 1968), p. 109.

[7]A. M. Ramsey, *The Resurrection of Christ* (London: Geoffrey Bles, 1945), p. 19.

Chapter 18

[1]Hodge, p. 635.

[2]John R. W. Stott, "The Great Commission," in *One Race, One Gospel, One Task,* World Congress on Evangelism, Berlin 1966, Official Reference Volumes, ed. Carl F. H. Henry and W. Stanley Mooneyham (Minneapolis: World Wide Publications, 1967), I, p. 46.

[3]Calvin, pp. 527-28.